SATHYA SAI VAHINI

[Spiritual Message of Sri Sathya Sai]

by

BHAGAWAN SRI SATHYA SAI BABA

PRASANTHI NILAYAM

SRI SATHYA SAI BOOKS & PUBLICATIONS TRUST
Prasanthi Nilayam - 515 134
Anantapur District, Andhra Pradesh, India.
STD: 08555 ISD: 91-8555
Phone : 287375 Fax : 287236

International Standard Book Number 81-7208-295-9

First Enlarged Edition : June, 2002
Reprint : August, 2004
Reprint : October, 2005
Reprint : April, 2007

Published by:
The Convener,
Sri Sathya Sai Books and Publications Trust
Prasanthi Nilayam, India - Pin Code 515 134.
STD: 08555 ISD: 91-8555
Phone: 287375 Fax: 287236
email: enquiry@sssbpt.org

Printed at:
Vipla Computer Services
(Designers & Multi Colour Offset Printers)
Nallakunta, Hyderabad - 500 044.
Ph. +91-40-27654003, 27676910

Dear Seeker!

Bhagawan has announced Himself as the Divine Teacher of Truth, Beauty and Goodness. By precept and example, through His writings and discourses, letters and conversations, He has been instilling the supreme wisdom and instructing all mankind to translate it into righteous living, inner peace and universal love. When the *Ramakatha Rasavahini*, the uniquely authentic nectarine stream of the Rama story, was serialised in full in the *Sanathana Sarathi,* Bhagawan blessed readers with a new series which He named *Bharathiya Paramartha Vahini* (The Stream of Indian Spiritual Values). While these precious essays on the basic truths, that foster and feed Indian culture since ages before history began, were being published, Bhagawan decided to continue the flow of illumination and instruction under a more comprehensive and meaningful name, *Sathya Sai Vahini*—the Ganga from the Lotus Feet of the Lord—"The

Flow of Divine Sai Grace." This book, therefore, contains the two Vahinis that have merged in one master stream.

Inaugurating these series, Bhagawan wrote, for publication in the *Sanathana Sarathi,* "Moved by the urge to cool the heat of conflict and to quench the agonising thirst for 'knowledge about yourself' that you are afflicted with, see, here it comes, the *Sathya Sai Vahini*, wave behind wave, with the *Sanathana Sarathi* as the medium between you and me." With infinite compassion, this Sathya Sai incarnation of the Omniwill is giving millions of persons in all lands freedom from disease, distress and despair, narcotics, narcissism and nihilism. He is encouraging those who suffer gloom through wilful blindness to light the Lamp of Love in order to see the world and the Lamp of Wisdom to see themselves. "This is a tantalising true-false world. Its apparent diversity is an illusion. It is One, but is cognised by the maimed multiple vision of humans as Many," says Bhagawan. This book is the twin Lamp He has devised for us.

Lord Krishna aroused Arjuna from the gloomy depression into which he led his mind, at the very moment when duty called on him to be himself—the far-famed warrior, ready and eager to fight on behalf of right against might. Krishna effected the cure by reminding him of the Atma which was his reality and of Himself being the Atma he was. Bhagawan says that we too are easily prone to get caught "in the coils of cleverness and the meshes of dialectical logic. The key to success in spiritual endeavour (and, what is life worth, if it is not dedicated to that high endeavour?) is philosophical inquiry and moral advance, both culminating in the awareness of the Atma, the source and sum of all the energy and activity that is." We are all motivated by fear, doubt and attachments as Arjuna was. We are all hesitant at the cross-roads between the this and That, the wave and the ocean.

But as created by Him, we are "the miracle of miracles." Bhagawan says, "Whatever is not in man cannot be anywhere outside him. Whatever is visible outside him is but a rough reflection of what really is in him." "The Atma is free. It is Purity. It is Fullness. It is unbounded. Its centre is the body but its circumference is beyond the beyond." Man has been endowed with a super intellect that can recognise the existence of the Atma, strive for bringing it into his awareness and succeed.

However, very few are human enough to seek to know who they are, why they are here and wherefrom, and whither they go from here. They move about with temporary names, encased in evanescent ever-changing bodies. So, Bhagawan accosts us, "Listen! Children of immortality, Listen! Listen to the message of the Rishis who had the vision of the Most Majestic Person, the *Purushotthama,* the Foremost and the First, who dwells beyond the realms of Illusion and Delusion. Oh ye Human beings! You are by nature ever full. You are indeed God moving on earth. Is there a greater sin than calling you 'sinners'? When you accept the appellation, you are defaming yourselves. Arise! Cast off the humiliating feeling that you are sheep. Do not be deluded into that idea. You are Atma. You are drops of *Amrith* (Divine immortality granting nectar), Immortal Truth, Beauty, Goodness. You have neither beginning nor end. All things material are your bond slaves. You are not their bond slaves, as you imagine now."

Bhagawan says, "Through the unremitting practice of Truth, Righteousness, and Fortitude, the Divinity quiescent in the individual has to be induced to manifest itself in daily living, transforming it into the joy of truly loving." "Know the Supreme Reality, breathe It. Bathe in It. Live in It. Then It becomes all of you and you become fully It." A material object is not self-expressive or *swathahprakaasa* (Self-luminance). It depends wholly on the capacity for knowledge or *chithsakthi* (power of consciousness, awareness) of the individualised Atma for its manifestation or *prakasa*. The relative world of objects is dependent upon the relative consciousness of the *Jivi* or individualised Atma. When the object is further scrutinised and the true basis of the plurality is grasped, Brahmam or the Oversoul as the First Principle is acknowledged as a logical necessity. Subsequently, when sense-control, mind-cleansing, concentration and inner silence are achieved, what appeared as a logical necessity dawns upon the purified consciousness as a Positive Permanent Impersonal Will (*Prajnaanam Brahma*), whose expression is all this.

Sathya Sai Vahini reveals to us in unmistakable terms that the self in man is "no other than the Overself or God."

We are told that this is true not only of mankind but of all beings, everywhere and anywhere. In fact, "Will causes this unreal multiplicity of Cosmos on the One that He is. He can by the same Will end the phenomenon." "Being (God) is behind the Becoming and Becoming merges in Being. This is the eternal Play," says Bhagawan.

As Bhagawan writes, "the supreme end of education, the highest purpose of instruction, is to help us to become aware of the universal immanent Impersonal." Sathya Sai in His role as the Teacher of Teachers is instructing us herein for this supreme adventure of the soul. Seekers proceeding on this pilgrimage have in Him a compassionate guide and guardian, for He is the embodiment of the very Will that planned the Play.

As we are led through the valley of this Vahini by Bhagawan who holds us by the hand, He exhorts us to admire, appreciate and adore the seers and sages of many lands who have pioneered into this realm and laid down limits and bounds, preparatory disciplines and practices, to smooth the path and hasten the discovery of Truth. He writes of the Vedas and later spiritual texts, of the forms of worship that have stood the test of centuries of loyal acceptance, and of the disciplinary codes laid down for the four stages of human life and for humans with pronounced inborn characteristics—the vertical uplifting *Sathwic*, the horizontal expansive *Rajasic* and the dull declining *Thamasic*. He clarifies the role of *Karma* and its consequence.

"Like a frail ship caught in a stormy sea, man climbs up a gigantic wave and reaches its froth-edged peak. The next moment, he is hurled into the trough, only to rise again. The rise and fall are both the consequences of his own deeds. They design the palace and the prison for man. Grief or joy is the resound, the reflection or reaction of one's own actions. The Jivi can escape both by cultivating the attitude of a witness, not involved in the activities he has to do." Bhagawan writes of *Yoga* as the process of the "coming together of *Jivatma* and *Paramatma*, the Self and the Overself" and He elaborates on the path of Love (*Bhakthi*), of selfless activity (Karma), of mastery over the mind (*Raja*), of sublimation of Consciousness (*Jnana*). Bhagawan analyses the rights and responsibilities of the individual and society and reveals to us that they have the one underlying purpose of spiritual fulfilment.

To sum up, the *Sathya Sai Vahini* is the Gita given to us by the Person who, as Sanathana Sarathi, eager and ready to hold the reins of our senses, mind, consciousness, ego and intellect, and guide us safely to Prasanthi Nilayam, the Abode of Supreme peace, the goal of all mankind.

May we all be blessed by His Love and Grace.

—N. KASTURI

✧ ✧ ✧ ✧ ✧

CONTENTS

✧ ✧ ✧ ✧ ✧

1. The Supreme Reality

The process of living has the attainment of the Supreme as its purpose and meaning. By the Supreme is meant the Atma. All those who have grown up in the *Bharathiya* (Indian) culture—the Bharathiyas—know that the Atma is everywhere. But when asked how they have come to know of this, some assert that the Vedas have taught them so, some others quote the Sastra texts, and some others rely on the experiential testimony of the great sages. Each of them bases his conclusions and proves its correctness according to the sharpness of his intellect. Many great men have directed their intelligence towards the discovery of the omnipresent Atma and succeeded in visualising that Divine Principle. In this country, *Bharath* (India), they have evidence of the successful realisation of the goals placed before themselves, by preachers, pundits, aspirants and ascetics, when they tried earnestly to pursue them. However, among millions of men, we can count only a few who have been able to visualise the Universal Atman.

No other living being has been endowed with the intelligence and discriminative faculty, heightened to this degree, in order to enable it to visualise the Atma. This is the reason why man is acclaimed as the crown of creation, and why the Sastras proclaim that the chance of being born as man is a very rare piece of good fortune. Man has the qualifications needed to seek the cause of Creation. He has in him the urge and the capacity. He is utilising the Created Universe for promoting his peace, prosperity and safety. He is using the forces and things in nature for promoting his happiness and pleasure. This is approved by the Vedas themselves.

The Vedas are the authority for the faith of millions. They are the very words of God. The Hindus believe that the Vedas had no beginning and will have no end. God speaks to man. They are not books written by authors. They are revelations conferred by God on many inquirers, of the ways of earning the Supreme Goal. They existed before they were revealed as valid paths. They will continue valid even if man forgets the path. They did not originate at any period of time nor can they be effaced at some other time. The *Dharma* (righteousness) which the Vedas allow us to glimpse is also without a beginning or an end. For, it refers to the Supreme Goal.

Of course, a few may argue that, though it may be conceded that the Dharma relating to the supreme goal has no ending, surely it must have had a beginning. The Vedas declare that the cycle of Creation—Dissolution has no point where it begins and no point where it ends. It is a continuous wheel. And there is no change in the quantum of the Cosmic Energy—either increase or decrease. It is ever the same, ever established in Itself. The Created and the Creator are two parallel lines with their beginnings unknown and their endings incomprehensible. They are moving at equal distances from each other, ever and ever. Though God is ever-active, His Will and the Power behind it are not clear to the human intellect.

The Supreme, according to the Bharathiyas, (inheritors of Indian culture) is Vastness Itself. It rises to the high skies and roams free in that expanse. It was declared in clear terms, long prior to the historical period. The study of the concept of the Supreme and the propagation of this concept suffered serious setbacks in the course of history. But it has confronted each of these with success and is today asserting itself, alive and alert. This is proof of the innate strength of this revelation. The conceptions of the Supreme Goal as laid down in Judaism, Christianity and Zoroastrianism endeavoured to subsume into their categories the Bharathiya concept and transfuse it as part of themselves; still, it did not accept an alien status in its own "birthplace." On the other hand, it clarified to those religions themselves their own concept of the Ultimate and emphasised the Unity of all viewpoints, and established cordiality on the basis of the absence of difference. While the stream of knowledge regarding the Supreme Goal discovered by the Bharathiya saints flowed on, the concepts of the other faiths remained as pools beside it.

In India (Bharath) itself many sects were born like mushrooms from out of the main faith. They tried to pluck by the roots or to cause mortal damage to the basic concept of Hinduism regarding the Reality, the Supreme. But as in a terrific quake of land, the waters of the sea recede only to return with thousand fold fury roaring back upon the shore it had seemed to quit. This stream of Bharathiya wisdom was restored to its pristine glory when it rose above the confusion and conflicts of history. When the agitations subsided, it attracted the varied sects that distracted the mind of man, and merged them into the expansive form. The Atma principle of the Bharathiyas is all-embracing, all-revealing, all-explaining and all-powerful.

Developing faith in the Atma Principle and loving it earnestly—this is the real worship. The Atma is the one and only Loved One for man. Feel that it is more loveable than any object here or hereafter—that is the true adoration man can offer to God. This is what the Vedas teach. The Vedas do not teach the acceptance of a bundle of frightfully hard rules and restrictions. They do not hold before man a prison house where man is shut in by the bars of cause and effect. They teach us that there is One who is the sovereign behind all these rules and restrictions, One who is the core of each object, each unit of energy, each particle or atom and One under whose orders alone the five elements—ether, air, fire, water and earth—do operate. Love Him, adore Him, worship Him—say the Vedas. This is the grand philosophy of Love as elaborated in the Vedas.

The supreme secret is that man must live in the world where he is born like the lotus leaf, which though born in water floats upon it without being affected or wetted by it. Of course, it is good to love and adore God with a view to gain some valuable fruit either here or hereafter. But since there is no fruit or object more valuable than God or more worthwhile than God, the Vedas advise us to love God, with no touch of desire in our minds. Love, since you must love for love's sake; Love God, since whatever He can give is less than He Himself. Love Him alone, with no other wish or demand.

This is the Supreme Teaching of the Bharathiyas. Dharmaraja, the eldest of the Pandava brothers, as depicted in the Mahabharatha, is the ideal of this type of Lover. When he lost to his enemies his vast empire, which *included* all India, and had perforce to live in caves among the Himalayan ranges, with his consort Droupadi, she asked him one day, "Lord! You are undoubtedly the topmost among those who follow unwaveringly the path of Dharma; yet, how is it that such a terrible calamity happened to you?" She was stricken with sorrow.

Dharmaraja replied, "Droupadi, do not grieve. Look at this Himalayan range. How magnificent! How glorious! How beautiful! How sublime! It is so splendid a phenomenon that I love it without limit. It will not grant me anything; but it is my nature to love the beautiful, the sublime. So, here too I am residing, with Love. The embodiment of this sublime beauty is God. This is the meaning and significance of the love for God.

"God is the only entity that is worth loving. This is the lesson that the age-long search of our Bharathiyas has revealed. This is the reason why I am loving Him. I shall not wish for any favour from Him. I shall not pray for any boon. Let him keep me where He loves to keep me. The highest reward for my love is His love, Droupadi! My love is not an article in the market." Dharmaraja understood that Love is a Divine quality and has to be treated so. He taught Droupadi that Love is the spontaneous nature of those who are ever in the awareness of the Atma.

The Love which has the Atma as its basis is pure and sublime. But since man is bound by various pseudo forms of love, he believes himself to be just a Jiva, isolated and individualised, and deprives himself of the fullness and vastness of Divine Love. Hence, man has to win the Grace of God. When he secures that Grace, the Jivi or the individual will be released from identification with body and can identify himself with the Atma. This consummation is referred to in the Vedas as "Liberation from Bonds" (*Bandha-*

vicchedana), or "Release" (*Moksha*). To battle against the tendency of body-identification, and to win the Grace of God as the only means of victory, spiritual exercises have been laid down, such as philosophical inquiry, besides sense-control (*dama*), and other disciplines of the sixfold *sadhana* (spiritual discipline). The practice of these will ensure the purification of the consciousness. It will then become like a clean mirror that can reflect the object, so the Atma will stand revealed clearly. For *Jnanasiddhi* (the attainment of the highest wisdom), *Chitthasuddhi* (the cleansing of the consciousness) is the Royal Path. For the pure in heart, this is easy of achievement. This is the central truth of the Indian search for the ultimate Reality. This is the very vital breath of the teaching.

The Bharathiya approach is not to waste time in discussions and assertions of faith in dogmas. They do not delight in the sight of empty oyster shells thrown upon the beach. They seek to gain the pearls that lie in the depths of the sea. They would gladly dive into those depths and courageously seek for pearls. The Vedas show them the ideal to follow and the road which leads to the realisation. The ideal is the awareness of the supreme Truth that lies beyond the knowledge gained by the senses of man. The Vedas remind man that the non-physical Atma is in the physical "him," that embodiment of Truth is the Supreme Atman, the *Paramatman*. That alone is real and permanent. The rest are all transitory, evanescent.

The Vedas took form only to demonstrate and emphasise the existence of God. The Hindu *siddhapurushas* (those who attain the highest goal of spiritual sadhana) have all travelled along the Vedic path and carried on their investigations according to Vedic teachings. The Sastras contain authentic versions of their experiences and the bliss they won. In the Sastras, and in the Upanishads, they assert, "We had the awareness of the Atma." Hindus do not aim at confronting a dogma or a theory and scoring a victory over it. They aim at testing that dogma or theory in actual practice. Their goal is not mere empty faith. It is the *Sthithi* (the stage reached), the *Siddhi* (the wisdom won). The life-aim of the Bharathiyas is to reach fulfilment, through constant sadhana, the fulfilment that comes from the awareness of one's divinity. Mergence with the Divine is the attainment of fullness. This is the Supreme Victory for the Hindu, the Bharathiya.

✧ ✧ ✧ ✧ ✧

2. From Truth To Truth

Questions may be asked, and doubts expressed by many, about the state of a person after he has attained fulfilment, the fullness of awareness. His life will be saturated with unexcelled *Ananda* (Divine bliss), and he will experience oneness of thought, emotion and knowledge with all. He will be in ecstasy, immersed in the One and Only, the Eternal Divine Principle, for that alone can confer joy during the process of living. Genuine joy is this and no other. God is the embodiment of eternal ever-full joy. Those loyal to Bharathiya culture, whatever the sect or faith which they claim as their special mould, accept this axiom, that "God is the highest source of joy." This *matha* (conclusion) they accept as *abhimatha* (dearest and most pleasurable).

Fullness means wholeness. Wholeness implies One and not two or three. There cannot then be any place for the individual. When an individualised Atma or Jivi, the particularised differentiated self, has become full and whole, there is no possibility of his return to the consciousness of the objective world. Some doubts may arise in the minds of many.

But this line of thought is not correct. When the individualised Jivi becomes fixed in the totality or *Samasthi* (the whole) he loses all ideas of distinction and is ever in the consciousness of the totality, the One that subsumes the many. He will then be aware that the reality of each is the reality of all and that Reality is the One Indivisible Atma. He will not exhibit any consciousness of distinction between individuals.

The Divine that he knows, as the core of each 'thing and being' is now recognised by him as the Divine that he himself is; and so he will be deeper than ever in the fullness of Ananda. How can he then experience separateness? No, he cannot. The rays of that Ananda illumine all regions. The sages and the great *Rishis* (One leading a life without desires) became aware of the Bliss. They communicated that experience to the world in easily understandable language. The unreachable moon is made known by pointing a finger in the direction where it can be seen! So too, they brought within the purview of men, according to the state of consciousness which each of them had attained, the Truth that lies beyond the reach of mind and speech. Their teachings were not only simple, but varied to educate and elevate all levels of understanding.

A small example:

One feels happy when one has the knowledge that this one little body is his, does he not? Then when he knows that two bodies are his, should he not be twice happy? In the same way, with the knowledge that he has an increasing number of bodies, the experience of happiness goes on increasing. When the whole world is known to be one body, and world-consciousness becomes part of the awareness, then the Ananda will be full. To get this multi-consciousness, the limited egocentric prison walls must be destroyed. When the ego-self identifies itself with the Jivi or Atma, death will cease. When the ego-self identifies itself and merges with the Bliss of the One, sorrow will cease. When it merges with Jnana or the Higher Wisdom, error will cease. "Material individualness is born out of delusion. This body which creates that impression is only an ever-evolving atom of a boundless ocean. The second entity in me is the other Form, namely, the embodied Self. When the ego of mine merges with the Self in me, then the delusion disappears, through the upsurge of its opposite knowledge." When man's thought matures in the process of time, undoubtedly all schools of thought have to reach this conclusion.

A tree's value is estimated, with reference to its fruits. Take idol-worship, for example. Moralists, metaphysicians, philosophers, adherents of the path of devotion, and the foremost among the virtuous in all parts of the world have all agreed that idol worship is highly beneficial. So long as attachment persists to the material body and possessions, worship of a material symbol is necessary. It is but a means. But many decry it as a superstition. This is not correct. It is not the right approach. Such an attitude is just an outburst of foolishness.

Is it not a fact that the belief in one's being the body, a superstition? Can the body last forever? Is it not a skin doll with nine apertures, in which life is so perilously existent that a sneeze can cause collapse? Again, should we not characterise the life people lead, believing in the reality of this world, as another superstition? Is not all the self-importance assumed by people who have positions of power and a great quantity of riches, another foolish pose? But acts done on the basis of faith in the Atma, the Reality within, cannot be dubbed as superstitious or foolish. For every opinion one expresses, if proper reasons are given, all will rejoice. But to declare as superstitious all that one does not like, is a sign of frenzy, foolishness or egoism.

We will find it impossible to love God or adore Him unless we meditate on some Form. This is as essential as breathing for sheer living. That is a necessary stage in the process of living. One has to accept it as such. Childhood is the father of old age. Can old age condemn childhood or teenage, as evil? To experience the Divine Principle, idol-worship *is* and *has been* a great help to many. How then can the aspirant and the practitioner of spiritual disciplines condemn idol-worship after passing through that stage and deriving benefits from it? That would indeed be very wrong and inappropriate.

The Bharathiya march towards the Supreme Reality is not from Untruth to Truth. It is from truth to Truth, from incomplete truth to complete Truth, from partial truth to full Truth. For what are sadhanas? Every effort made by men, from the remote forest-dwellers and the unsophisticated tribals, who adore the gross forms of Divinity, to those highly evolved seekers who adore the Full and the Absolute, is a sadhana. Each such effort will take man a step forward in progress.

Each individual Jivi is comparable to a bird. It can, by longer and higher flights, rise up into the sky. And a stage may finally be gained when it can fly right up to the full-splendoured orb of the Sun.

The basic truth of Nature is the One in the Many. That is the key to its understanding. The Bharathiyas grasped this truth. They held fast to this key. People of other countries were content to lay down certain axioms and enforce belief in them. They insisted on the acceptance of these axioms and the observance of rules and regulations that arise out of them. They held one single coat before the individuals of the society where they lived and required everyone to wear that same coat. If it did not suit the size of anyone, there was no alternative coat for such people. They had to live without a coat to protect them against the chill wind.

The Bharathiya approach was quite different. For each aspect or variation of feeling and thinking, volition and action, they made available a distinct Name and Form, and provided modes of worship and ways of adoration, in accordance with the emotional needs and intellectual calibre of the aspirants and devotees. Of course, a few had no need for such special consideration and treatment. But many took advantage of this concession, and advanced in their march towards wisdom and liberation.

For one thing, never was it laid down as part of the Bharathiya spiritual endeavour, that idol-worship is a must or that it is a stage that has to be gone through. But there is one fact which each one must preserve in his memory. It is this: Bharathiyas may have attachment to their bodies. They may be attached to the upkeep and development of their standards of living, but they would never yearn to cut the throats of others. The Bharathiya who is fanatic about his religion would rather immolate himself in flames raised and fed by himself, rather than, through hatred, burn alive those who do not accept and revere his religion. Bharathiya spiritualism negated the destruction of the Atma, the One inextinguishable Truth.

For the Bharathiya religion fostered the faith that the Self in man is no other than the Overself or God. Bharathiya religion directs a long journey by men and women, through varied paths, confronted and controlled by varied circumstances but encouraged and enlightened by various types of faith, towards the goal of the splendour of God-consciousness or the Consciousness of the Divine. Though the practices and rites might appear on the surface to be crude, they are not opposed to the ultimate Truth. The seeming contradictions have to be interpreted as incidental to the need to inspire people with varied intellectual, moral, economic and social backgrounds. For example, the light that comes through a tiny piece of coloured glass is of the same origin as bigger, clearer light. The extent, clarity, brightness, etc. of light depends on the medium only. The source of all light is the One Truth, the Source of All, the Basis of All, the Goal of All, the Reality in All, and the Centre in All. As the thread on which pearls are strung as a rosary, God or the Overself is interpenetrative in all beings. In *all* beings—that is the message of Bharath, all beings everywhere, anywhere!

Examine carefully all the texts and scriptures that deal with Bharathiya culture and traditions. Find out whether in any of them there is mention that Moksha or Liberation or the Highest Realisation is available to those who are Bharathiyas *only,* and not to others. Can you produce a single statement on those lines? It can be emphatically asserted that you cannot discover a statement like that. Bharathiya Spiritualism has limitless vastness, and immensely high ideals. It is a full stream of sanctifying ideations, flowing along with no decline or diminution, straight and smooth to the Ocean of Divine Grace. The journey is direct, along a royal road towards the supreme Goal.

Another point: The source of all spiritual principles recognised and revered by Bharathiyas is God. He is the one supporting Pillar. Therefore, no other support is needed for faith. Bharathiya spiritualism is the very foundation of all other faiths. It stands on the very summit. It has achieved victory over many opposing faiths, confronting them with many valid arguments and theories. Bharathiyas have no need to follow any religion or spiritual discipline, besides their own. For nowhere else can you secure a discipline or truth that is not existing herein. Other faiths have only adopted some one or other of its beliefs and principles and placed them before people as ideals to be adopted.

What has to be borne in mind is this: Bharathiya texts on spiritualism are the most ancient in the whole world. They are the earliest studies and discoveries of the Atma, on Personal and Impersonal God, and on Codes of Conduct, individual and social, based on those revelations and discoveries. In no other country, among no other peoples have such ancient teachings seen the light. There may be perhaps, some misty ideas or brief glimpses; but they do not deserve the name, spiritual text or literature. The Vedic literature pictures not only spiritual inquiries by the sages and *Sadhakas* (Spiritual aspirants) and their results, but also, their lines of thought, their yearnings and aspirations, their secular struggles and temporal problems.

✧ ✧ ✧ ✧ ✧

3. The One Alone

The very first experience in the history of Indian thought is the thrill of wonder. This is expressed in the *Rks* or hymns found in *Rig Veda*, the earliest revelations of the Bharathiya mind. The Rks are all about the Gods or the Shining Ones (the *Devas*). Of these Devas, there are many; Indra, Varuna, Mitra, Parjanya—these are the names of a few. They appear in these Rks, one after the other. Of these, Indra with the Thunderbolt (*vajra*) as his weapon is the chief. He is the mighty One who confers rain upon the earth. Indra is called so, since he is the Master of the *Indriyas* (the senses) of man, that is to say, he is the Mind which handles the senses. He is also known as *Puruhutha—puru* meaning "often" and *hutha*, "invited"—the entire name meaning, "the God who is most called upon." The Mind (which is identified with Indriyas, since it masters them) is also adored in the Vedas as Rudra. The Mind contacts the objective world and experiences it through the instrumentality of the five senses. This aspect of the Mind is the Indra aspect. It has also another capability. It can master the senses, and become aware of the Universal Inner Truth of the multiplicity called the Objective world. This aspect of the Mind is designated as "Rudra." This is the reason why the Vedas describe Indra and Rudra as the One with two names.

About the other Gods too, it is possible to quote many such descriptions. Yet ultimately, all descriptions lead to the same conclusion. The Rks adore Deities, first, as presiding over some function or other. Then, these latter get transformed into different names and forms of the One God who has all the worlds in Itself, who is the Witness, resident in all hearts, and who is the Sovereign of all Creation. Gradually, all other meanings and reactions are suppressed, as not relevant. For example, an element of fear is associated with the deity, Varuna. The fear sprouts and spreads in some Rks, but soon, the wisdom of the *Aryas* (Noble seekers) subjugates the fear. Many Rks are prayers to Varuna from people afraid of being punished by Him for their sins. But the idea of a terrorising God cannot flourish on Indian soil. Nor can many Gods of many natures. Bharathiya culture and spiritual outlook upheld the One God or Easwara.

Next, the *Ekeswara*!(One God) This axiom, that there can be only One and not many, is current in India from very ancient times. Even in the ancient Vedic and Samhitha literature, this faith is already evident as an age-long belief.

But the notion of a personal God struck the thinkers and practitioners of this land as rather elementary, a kind of unripe stage in spiritual progress. It did not satisfy their highest aspirations. This attitude found in the revelations of Rishis has not been understood or appreciated by scholars and writers of other countries who have studied and commented on the Vedas and affiliated texts. They still dwell on the earlier belief in "many gods" or the later belief in "one personal God." Ignorance of this kind brings a smile to the lips of the Hindu.

Really speaking, even those who learn in their mothers' laps to put faith in a God equipped with attributes, known by a name and having a recognisable Form, have later to rise up to a stage higher than this and become aware of the One, that is spoken of as "having many names and many forms." The sadhanas (spiritual practices) are directed to the realisation of this Truth.

The ONE—in Him alone is all this flux, all this changing Cosmos, established. He is the guide and guardian of every consciousness. All such denotations touch only the fringe of the ONE. Westerners said that the intelligence of man can succeed in this venture. But the seekers of this land showed a heroism that could not be measured or limited. This is a fact that cannot but be accepted. Western Philosophers renowned for their daring flights into the realms of the spirit have shown only a tiny spark of this heroism. So, they are amazed at the speculative and experiential heights reached by the sages of India. This feeling of wonder has been charmingly expressed by Professor Max Mueller. "Into whatever unknown realms of experience their causative and positive inquiry led them, the Indian seekers ventured boldly therein. They never hesitated to discard, for the sake of success in this adventure, whatever they felt as an encumbrance. They were not affected by fear of how others might judge them." Max Mueller exhorted people to involve themselves in Bharathiya *Paramartha Vahini*, (the Nectarine stream of the search for the Supreme, flowing in India), for he felt the Indian Sadhakas pursued the path of Right, the path of Truth.

Ekam sath; vipraah bahudhaa vadanthi. (One alone is; the wise speak of It as many). This indeed is most sublimely meaningful. This is the basic truth behind the spiritual efforts of India since ages. Even the theistic principle and practice that will spread all over the world with unprecedented benediction in the coming years have as their basis this great axiom laid down by the sages of India, long, long ago.

Rks arose on various Deities and Divine Forces, because the Rishis knew that the "One that alone is," can be cognised by each one only from his own viewpoint, and that it is different for different persons, depending on the stage reached in clarifying and purifying the vision. They announced, through that statement, their discovery that the One is the subject which all the sages and saints, seers and poets, hymnists and composers adored and praised in various languages, during various moods, through various styles of expression. Thus, from the declaration quoted above "*Ekam sath; vipraah bahudhaa vadanthi,*" emerged consequences of the highest value to the world. For example, many are surprised that India is the one country where religious fanaticism is absent and no one hinders or harms the religious observances of another. There are, in this country, theists, atheists, dualists, non-dualists, monotheists and others. They all live together in peace and harmony, without causing or suffering injury.

Materialists stood on the steps of temples (held sacred by Brahmins and resorted to by them for worship) and defamed and denied God. They called upon all to follow them. They declared that the idea of God is but an insane fancy. They condemned God, scriptures, codes of morality, righteousness and guiding principles and said that they were all superstitions designed and developed for selfish aggrandisement by the Brahmins. They roamed across the land and propagated these conclusions. And no one hindered them. Buddhism, which systematically slighted Hindu rites and religious beliefs was allowed to coexist in an atmosphere of respect. The Jains too did not accept the Vedas and the Vedic Gods. They asked in derision how such Gods can exist and be believed in. Examples of the spirit of tolerance rooted in the revelatory statement quoted above are innumerable. Until the ravaging Muslims sprang on this country, no one in this land of Bharath knew what was meant by violence. It is only when foreign hordes fell upon them and resorted to violence that the people came to know how intolerant man can be.

Hindus helped Christians to build churches in India. They showed readiness to cooperate with Christians. This is evident all over the country. There was no bloodshed, at any time, in dealing with Christians. The stream of thought directed to the supreme Truth would not allow itself to be polluted by violence. To confirm this fact as well as to understand the validity of this attitude requires clear thinking and strength of intellect.

Buddhists who were the very first propagators of religion, spread their faith by travelling over the world. That religion entered all countries famed in those days as civilised. The monks who ventured into those lands were tortured. Hundreds were killed by imperial decree. But soon, good fortune smiled on Buddhism. Buddhism taught that violence has to be eschewed. Buddha was accepted as a God, as another Name for the One, which has many names, according to the Vedic dictum, "*Ekam sath, vipraah bahudhaa vadanthi*." He was Indra, He was Rudra. That was the unifying effect of the basic revelation of the sages. May this declaration be ever in the memory of man!

Bharathiyas, grown up in the culture of India, have deep faith in the equality of all faiths. Whether it is Hinduism, Buddhism, Islam, Zoroastrianism or Christianity, they believe that no one should talk lightly of the worship of God. They believe that when anyone talks lightly on any One of the Names of God or any of the Forms of God whom others adore, they are insulting the One God. This was the message held forth by the Indian way of spiritual life. Those who have learnt this truth and adhere to it are the real sons and daughters of India.

This Truth is beyond the grasp of all. Not all can achieve this knowledge: who is the ruler of the Universe? Who is it that stands outside it and guides it? What is the cause of the existence of this Cosmos? Whence did this originate? How did it happen? What caused this existence? The Vedas have many Rks dealing with these mysteries. Bharathiyas have probed into them.

Creation involves the putting together of substances. What is put together must come apart, in course of time and get liberated. The individual is created and so he has to disintegrate and die. Now some are born happy. Some are enjoying healthy, happy lives. Some are born miserable. Others are born without hands or legs. Some are born feebleminded or as defectives. Who hurt them or injured them? God is proclaimed as just and kind. It can be argued: how can such a God ever be so partial and prejudiced? How can such differential treatment come into the Realm ruled by God? Such doubts are natural. But the vision of the sages of Bharath who moulded the thought of this land revealed to them that God is not the cause of these differences. They are the consequences of the acts indulged in by the individual in lives previous to the present one. They result in happiness and misery, health and handicaps.

Good and bad are self-made, the effects of what was done in previous lives. Can the bodies of men and their conditions, the ups and downs men meet in life, can they not be the accumulated result of hereditary impacts and tendencies? There are two things that stand like parallel lines before us, when we consider this subject, mental and material. If satisfactory solutions can be found for the problems relating to human nature and its special qualities in materialism, then there can be no basis for believing that there is a factor called Atma or the Soul! But it is impossible to demonstrate that the capacity to think, for example, has evolved out of physical matter.

When an item of work is done again and again, it becomes a habit, a skill; is it not? Therefore, the skill or habit that a new-born exhibits must be due to constant repetition indulged in long ago. Of course, such practice must have taken place in a previous life or many lives. So, it is necessary to posit the validity of the belief in past and future lives, for all living beings. This is a basic belief in Bharathiya spiritual thought.

✧ ✧ ✧ ✧ ✧

4. The Miracle Of Miracles

The children of Bharath (Bharathiyas) believe that they are, each one, the Atma. They are aware that the Atma cannot be cut in twain by the sword, that fire cannot burn It, that water cannot wet It, and that the wind cannot dry It. The Atma has no bounds. Its centre is in the body, but Its circumference is nowhere. Death means the Atma has shifted from one body to another. This is the belief that every Indian has firmly in mind.

The Atma is not subject to material or worldly limitations or laws. By Its very nature, It is Free. It is Unbounded. It is Purity. It is Holiness. It is Fullness. But since It is associated with material, inert bodies, It imagines that It is also a product of material composition. This is the wonder, the mystery, the miracle that It manifests! To unravel this mystery, and explain this miracle are beyond the capacity of anyone.

How could the Full (*Poorna*) Atma get entangled in the delusion that It is "not-full" (*apoorna*) "a fraction," "incomplete"? Some persons might charge the Bharathiyas, who declare that the awareness of incompleteness itself can never arise, as persons attempt to wriggle out of an impossible situation. They might say that this is but a stratagem to cover up their ignorance of the Truth. How can the Pure, the Unpartitionable, lose Its nature to the slightest extent? The Bharathiyas are simple and sincere, and their nature is seldom artificial. They would never attempt to wriggle out of a situation by resorting to specious arguments. They have the courage to encounter, in a manly way, any problem before them. Therefore, the answer to the question posed is: The delusion cannot happen! There is no basis for the error of imputing "incompleteness" for the "complete." The "full" entity called Atma can never imagine Itself as "wanting" or "less-than-full" or feel that It is limited or controlled by the material sheath whose core It is.

Every person knows that he feels he is the body. Can anyone announce how this feeling arose and persisted? No one can offer to answer this question. For to say, as some do, that it is the will of God, is no answer at all. The plain statement, "I do not know" conveys the same meaning, as the statement, "It is the will of God." One is no wiser at the latter statement than after hearing the first. What remains is this: "The Atma in the Individual, the Jivatma, is Eternal, Immortal, Full: There is no Death. What appears so is the shifting of Its centre."

Our present condition and circumstances are decided by the deeds done in previous lives. In a similar manner, the conditions in which we have to spend the future are determined by what we are doing now. Between one life and another, one death and the next, the individual either progresses or regresses, expands or shrinks. Like a frail ship caught in a stormy sea, man climbs the froth-rimmed peak of some gigantic wave, and the next moment, he is hurled with terrific speed into the deepest trough. The rise and the fall result inevitably from his good deeds and bad. Oh ye Children of Immortality! Listen! Listen to the answer given in the message of the Rishis who had the Vision of the Most Majestic of Persons, the *Purushottama*, (best among men and gods) who dwells beyond the realms of Delusion and Darkness: "Oh, Ye Human Beings! Brothers! For you to liberate yourselves from the succession of deaths, the only means is 'knowing Him.' Do not imagine that you are sinners, for you are heirs to eternal Ananda. You are 'images' of God, sharers in the undiminishable Ananda. You are by nature holy, ever-full. You are indeed God, moving on earth. Is there a sin greater than calling such as you, sinners? You are dishonouring yourselves, defaming yourselves, when you acknowledge the appellation, 'sinners.' Arise! Cast off the feeling that you are sheep. Do not be deluded into that idea. You are Atmas. You are drops of Amrith of Immortality, that know neither beginning nor end. All things material are your bond slaves, you are not *their* bond slaves."

These are the words of the Rishis. How can those who have not themselves delved into this Truth appreciate this Bharathiya interpretation? Indians are the fortunate ones who have achieved great strength in spirit, holding God as father, mother, guru, friend, and the beloved. They have adored God as dearer to them than anything or anyone, here or hereafter. How can those who are aware only of mere sensual pleasure know this supreme Truth? The craving for sensual pleasure veils the truth from the inner eye. That craving manifests in multiple ways, creating more and more desires and laying down more and more urges to action. These hide the truth like a thick curtain.

The recognition of this curtain is a big stage in spiritual progress. This is the *Maya* Principle of Vedantha. From immemorial times, though the Truth was self-evident, this curtain has hidden it from man. This has been discovered as the prime obstacle by Indians, since ages. How to remove the curtain and cognise the Truth? Indians knew that the solution does not lie in the objective, external world, and so, it would be futile to seek it there. The search in the external world, even for ages, cannot ensure success. For experience alone can guarantee conviction.

To gain experience, Indians entered into austerities and disciplined inquiry, until they "identified" the Truth, and announced it to the world. They discarded the urges of the senses and the manifold attractions of active involvement in the objective world. They taught the world this lesson. The mind of man was the instrument for the Indian seekers to discover this secret, which is the basic principle of Wisdom as treasured by them. It became imperative for them to use the mind itself and study its nature and characteristics. They realised soon enough that the study of the external world led them nowhere. They diverted their attention to the internal "regions" of their consciousness. Thus they laid the foundation for the Vedantic structure; this was the beginning of the Vedantic inquiry.

There is no need to seek Truth anywhere else. Seek it in man himself: he is the miracle of miracles. Whatever is not in man cannot be anywhere outside him. What is visible outside him is but a rough reflection of what really is in him! The ancient belief was that Easwara (God) ruled over the World, with Himself being outside it. This, the Indian seekers put to test through sadhana and revealed that God was and is in the world and of it. This is the first contribution of Indians to the spiritual world—that God is not external to man, but his very inner core. They declared that it is impossible to remove him from the heart where He has installed Himself. He is the very Atma of our Atma, the soul of our soul. He is the inner Reality of each.

Those who desire to grasp the supreme vision of Vedantic philosophy have to understand a few fundamental ideas. Philosophy is neither a book nor the work produced by one person. The supremely great Manu has named this Bharath as *Brahmavartha*, the Region of Brahma, the spiritual area where the quest of the ONE immanent and transcendent Principle originated and succeeded. The festive cavalcade of saints engaged in the quest began its march over the continents from this Bharath itself. Like mighty rivers from huge mountain ranges, the stream of spiritual sadhana for the discovery of the Higher Truth sprang from this land itself. This land has announced to the world its Spiritual Message with the confidence and courage of thunderblasts emanating from the womb of clouds. When inimical forces blasted into Bharath, this holy land bore the brunt of the blow. It had to present its heroic chest before the attack and absorb the initial impact. Many times this land had to bear these invading thrusts and suffer fierce injuries. But yet, this land has not fully lost its fame and glory and its steadfast strength on this path.

From this land, the Embodiment of Equanimity and Compassion, Nanak the Great, preached his highly wonderful message of Love. His all-embracing heart blossomed in this land. The Bharathiyas, Children of this Land, Inheritors of this Culture, spread their arms to receive in loving embrace not only the Hindu world but the Islamic world too. Among those who shone as heroic supporters of the Hindu culture unto the last, the foremost was Guru Govind Singh. Undeterred by tortures that forced him to shed his own blood and the blood of his own beloved, deserted by those for whom he had undergone such torture, he did not utter a word of blame against his compatriots, but, entered the Deccan and gave up his life, as the King of

Beasts does when his heart is hurt. May that great person's fame persist for ever on earth! Such eminent leaders render the whole of mankind indebted to them, for they serve the best interests of all men everywhere.

As each individual is a unique entity, so each nation too has a unique individuality. Each person is different from others in certain matters and is endowed with some special characteristics which are his own. So too, each nation has certain special features, not found in others. Each individual has to play a role as part of the system. His own previous Karma or activity has determined a special line or path for him. The history of nations too is the same. Each has to play a role already laid down by its destiny. Each nation has to deliver a special message of its own to the world community. Therefore, it is important that Bharathiyas must recognise, before everything else, the role that this nation has to play, the tune it must sing in the World Orchestra of Peace and Bliss. You must have heard, while listening to childhood tales, that there are gemstones in the hoods of some serpents and that, so long as those gems embellish the hoods, it is not possible to kill those serpents. Keep this story in your memory; then, you can understand the most miraculous event in human history, the survival of Bharathiya Spiritual Culture.

✧ ✧ ✧ ✧ ✧

5. Basic Belief

The Sanathana Dharma had to meet the determined opposition from Islam for centuries; political subjection to Muslim dynasties added to the problems. The cry, "Allaho-Akbar" rose to the skies, and challenged the very existence of the Bharathiya Culture that had been fostered since ages by seers. No other nation suffered so long and so deep from such fear. But the eternally fresh and vital Dharma of this land has stood the test and even today, Sanathana Dharma is as potent and valid as ever. It is ready to meet any challenge from any new quarter. From the signs of the times, it is evident that this culture is today dominant and powerful. Why, it is prepared even to march forward and expand its area of constructive influence. Expansion is the sign of "life," is it not?

This day the principles and practices laid down in Bharathiya Culture and the attitudes and feelings enshrined in it, are not lying low within the boundaries of this subcontinent. Whether we like it or not, they cross over to other lands and establish themselves there. The main ideas, the essential outlooks, penetrate the literature of those peoples and permeate their thought processes. In some lands, among some peoples, they have won even dominant roles, with no opposition. For, Bharath is offering as its contribution to the peace and prosperity of the World, an invaluable body of spiritual wisdom. This contribution is more elevating than that from any other country. It is more necessary, more basic and more precious than what any other nation can give. This fact is becoming clearer to all mankind.

The ancients of this land were not averse to the examination of other problems too. They tried, like other peoples, to unravel the mysteries of external Nature. And this amazing nation achieved results even in this field, through the exercise of their sharp intellect, which are beyond the fondest dreams of men in other countries.

The supreme end of education, the highest purpose of instruction, is to make man aware of the "universal immanent Impersonal." This is the truth that is loudly proclaimed in the Vedas. The seers and sages of Bharath courageously entered upon this adventure. The ever-changing aspects of Nature, the appearance and disappearance of its working, may be a fine subject for study. But the ancients of Bharath proclaimed that the science of the Transcendent Principle that permeates the Universe, the Unchanging Eternal, the Embodiment of Everlasting Ever-full Ananda, the Residence of Unaffected, Undiminished Peace, the Ultimate Refuge for all Time of the Individual Jivi, that science is the highest knowledge that man must gain.

The knowledge of the principles governing objective nature can at best provide man with food and clothing. It teaches man ways and means of gaining them. It leads to the exploitation of the weak by the strong. If the people of Bharath had bent their energies towards the discovery of the secrets of the world, they could have easily acquired mastery.

But very soon, the people of Bharath recognised that this search was but secondary and that the prime position should be assigned to the spiritual. They decided that pursuing the secrets of external nature was not the real sign of Bharathiya. This resolution brought glory to this nation. Others cannot even approach the fringe of this problem. Like Prahlada, of the legends, Indians have been able to survive ordeals of fire and escape unhurt the torture of ages. Those who had no spiritual outlook or aspiration were not reckoned as Bharathiyas. Many in foreign lands believed that Indians were more politically minded, an inference that was misleading. They felt that only a small fraction of Indians were spiritually-oriented. But Bharath always insisted that a spiritually directed way of life was the first and foremost duty of every Indian. Whenever the chance offered itself, after discharging this duty, Indians felt that they should collect and confirm the spiritual potency that they had. This was exactly what happened in the past.

National integration meant, in those days, the concentration and commingling of all the spiritual forces and urges that were scattered among seekers all over the land. The word, "nation," meant in India the grouping together of hearts that beat time to the same song and that respond, by similar vibration, to the same spiritual call. The basic truths that this faith expounded were as broad as the sky, as eternal as Creation. Those Truths were described in many subtle ways and commented upon very close and deep. But as a result of the very breadth of the vision that discovered them, and laid them down, it was inevitable that many faiths emanated on the basis of the beliefs they encouraged.

Diversities in attitudes and practices are natural and ought to be welcomed. There is no need for an ironclad hard Faith. Only there is no place for one- overall Faith. Rivalry among those following different paths cannot bring peace and prosperity to any country. Without the freedom to adopt faith, the world cannot progress. India taught that a small group can never command the inexhaustible resources of the world, that for the effective functioning of the community it is necessary to divide the work of the community among sections of the people, and allot the task of contributing its share of the common good to each section of the community. This gave facilities for diversities and for mutuality. Diversities were approved for the sake of the practical application of spiritual powers and potentialities. So, there is no need for factionalism and fights. The diversities too are but superficial. They are not really real. There is an entrancing sense of mystery that can explore these diversities and discover the key to visualise the ONE that underlies the many. his is what the ancient texts proclaim as the most precious revelation. "*Ekam sath, vipraah bahudha vadanthi*" (The One alone exists; wise men describe It in manifold ways).

Therefore, it can be asserted that the Faith of the Bharathiyas is the one Faith that accepts and reveres all Faiths. When we shelter factionalism and fanaticism in our hearts, in relation to our own specific faith or the faith of others, we, as descendants of those fathers are bringing disgrace on ourselves. Whether we are adhering to the classical Vedantic faiths or whether we are adopting recent trends in that Vedantic thought, we have to bear in mind certain basic universally accepted truths. All those who bear the name, Hindu, have to believe in them and shape their lives accordingly. May they have the will to do so.

1. The first of these is: "Bharathiyas do not insist that everyone has to be bound to one attitude, or that everyone must abide by one interpretation or commentary only, to the exclusion of other possible explanations or points of view, or that the way of life

with all its implications has to be the one approved by some one individual or group." The Bharathiya culture lays down that it is a heinous sin to exercise force upon anyone, in matters of the spirit.

2. Next: The Eternal Universal Dharma or Religion is taught by the Vedas. The sacred body of teachings, referred to as Vedic, is coeval with Creation, without ascertainable beginning or end. With it, all inquiry into the spirit and the ramifications of faith have to find fulfilment and close. One cannot escape this conclusion if he studies and practises the Vedas. For all problems involving differences in spiritual attitudes and aspirations, we can get solutions that are convincing from the Vedic texts themselves. The viewpoints differ about what portions of the Vedas are authoritative for each. Persons affiliated to one sect might regard some portions of the Vedas as holier and more sacrosanct than others. In spite of this, all are brothers and co-sharers of the teachings and the lessons imparted by the Vedas. All that is elevating and beneficial for us today, all that is holy and sacred to us, all that is pure and ennobling, have been made available to us from and through these wondrous texts of old. So long as we hold to this latter belief and proclaim it aloud, what can little differences of opinion over matters of minor importance do to cause rifts? For this reason, we have to announce these lessons and principles so that they spread beyond all horizons.

3. The Vedas are concerned with and they expound the Supreme Person, the Easwara who created this Universe, who fosters It, in whom It merges in accordance with the process of time, and in whom is again manifest as His Form this amazing Universe. We might have diverse beliefs about the nature and characteristics of this Easwara. One person might picture Him as having human nature and characteristics. Another might believe that He is the embodiment of non-human attributes, formless, Easwara. Every one of these can find in the Vedas declarations supporting his viewpoints. It is a fact that, though they hold diverse views, they all have faith in Easwara, the Godhead. That is to say, they believe that there is undoubtedly One transcendent eternal Power, and that all this has originated from It, and that all this has to merge in It again. This belief is the hallmark of a Bharathiya. He who has not acquired this belief is not entitled to the name, Bharathiya. He does not deserve to be called a Hindu.

Of what nature, with what characteristics is the Easwara you teach? This question is irrelevant to us. It is not so important. Let us not dispute about the various points of view that divide persons. Enough for us if Easwara is accepted and emphasised. For even though one description and delineation might be better and clearer than another, no delineation and description can be "bad." One declaration would be "good," the second one would be "better" and the third one, "best." But in the stream of Bharathiya spiritual adventure, no description or picturization can be pronounced "bad and unacceptable." That is the reason why Easwara confers Grace on all those who teach any Name and any Form that can attract and inspire man, as sacred and valid. May this faith grow from more to more. For, it brings more spiritual progress, the more it is acted upon. Only, the aspiration must be related to God or Easwara.

4. For spiritual exploration and discovery, there can be no qualification like wealth or disqualification like poverty. This truth has to be handed down to the children by Bharathiya parents. They have to grow up with this broad feeling.

5. Bharathiyas do not accept the belief, held by persons belonging to other countries, that the Universe was manifested a few thousand years ago and that it will be destroyed finally and forever, at some future date. Bharathiyas will not accept the theory that the Universe arose out of Nothing. They believe the Universe or this objective Creation is beginningless and endless, and that, according to the laws of evolution in time, it will recede from the gross into the subtle stage, and after being in that stage for some period, it will again recede into the causal stage from which It emerged. From the One into which it merges, it will gradually manifest itself as Many, through the subtle and the gross stages of expression.

✧ ✧ ✧ ✧ ✧

6. Religion Is Experience

This wave-like movement of proceeding and receding, of merging and emerging, has been happening since Time; it will happen till Time ends; it is eternal in its feature—this is the belief of Bharathiyas. Man is not just this gross body; in it, there is a subtle component called mind; inside it, as its prompter and spring, there is an even more subtle principle called the Jivatma (individualised Soul). This Jivatma has neither beginning nor end, it knows no death, it has no birth. This is the basis of the Bharathiya faith.

One other article of faith: This is a unique feature of Bharathiya mental equipment. Until the individualised soul gets liberated from the individualisation and merges in the Universal, thus attaining Moksha or liberation, it has to encase itself in one body after another, and go through the process called living. This idea is held by no other people. This is the *Samsara* idea, which the ancient texts or Sastras of India reveal and propagate. Samsara means "the movement into one form after another." All the different schools and sects among the Bharathiyas accept this fact that the Atmas (apparently individualised) are eternal and incapable of being affected by change. They may differ in describing or denoting the relationship between the Atma and Easwara or God. One school of thinkers may posit that the two are ever separate. Another may declare that the Jivatma is a spark in the universal flame of fire that Easwara is. A third may assert that the two are undifferentiated. But the truth remains that the Atma is beginningless and endless; since it is not born, it has no death. Its individualised image has to evolve through a series of bodies, until it attains fulfilment in the human. All schools are one in upholding this faith, in spite of the variety of their other interpretations.

We shall now come to the foremost among the glorious Truths, the most astounding of the basic Truths that the human intellect has attained in the spiritual field: the Atma is by its very nature, Purity, Fullness and Bliss (*Parisuddha* [absolute purity], *Paripoorna* [absolute fullness] and Ananda). This is the belief that animates all schools of thought, whether they are the worshippers of Sakthi, or Shiva, or Vishnu, or whether they are Buddhists or Jains. Every Hindu acknowledges it. The *Dwaithins* (dualists) believe that the fundamental, genuine nature of the Atma is Ananda; this is diminished and desiccated by the consequences of human actions, in life after life and therefore, has to be restored and revitalised by the Grace of God. The Adwaithins (the Monists) believe that there can be no diminution or desiccation. They assert that the Atma is fully splenderous; only, through the influence of the deluding effect of ignorance (Maya) which superimposes false impressions on what is really true, it appears as if it has diminished. Whatever may be the differences in interpretation, when we take our stand on the central core of the Truth on which all agree, between the "East" and the "West," there will be discerned a vast deep passage, where both do journey to the goal. The people of the Eastern countries seek in the inner regions of their selves the realisation of this gloriously beneficent consummation. While worshipping, we close the eyes and endeavour to visualise God inside ourselves. People of the West lift up their faces and visualise God in outer space, in the beyond. They believe that their scriptures have been recorded by Persons under the direction of God. Bharathiyas believe that the Vedas—their sacred scriptures—were the very breath of God conveying meanings to the sages who had installed Him in their hearts.

There is another point which we have to understand: We have to hold fast to it always. Unless a belief is held unshaken throughout night and day, it cannot be used to achieve victory. No success is possible otherwise. When a person asserts that he is low and mean and that he knows but little, he becomes low and mean and his knowledge shrinks. We become what we believe we are. We are the children of Almighty God, endowed with supreme Power, Glory and Wisdom. We are Children of Immortality. When we dwell in this thought, how can we ever be low and ignorant? Bharathiya spiritual culture enjoins on everyone to believe that the real nature of man is supreme and that he should ever be conscious of this truth.

The Bharathiyas of past ages had faith in their great Reality. They achieved victory in their endeavours as a result of this faith and rose to lofty heights. They reached the peak of progress. We have slid down into the present decline, mainly because we have lost faith in the Atma in us. This was the beginning of our fall. For, loss of confidence in the Atma or Self involves loss of faith in God Himself. That Omnipresence, that Inner Motivator of all, who is the warp and woof of our body and mind, our emotions and intellect—strengthening faith in Him is the only means of realising the highest goal of man. This is the lesson that Bharathiya spiritual history longs to teach.

Children of Bharath! Teach your children this life-preserving, glorious and heart-expanding Truth from the early days of life. The sanctifying vision that Bharathiyas secured is this: the Atma is full and free. It is a wonderful discovery, a thrilling thought! The Atma is by its very nature full; fullness need not be attained or accomplished and added to It. If fullness is added to it, it can also be subtracted by the passage of time, what is built up must disintegrate. If man is impure by nature, even though he may succeed in achieving purity for five minutes, he has to wallow later in impurity, for the purity that comes in the middle will be easily swept away by circumstances. So all Bharathiya spiritual thinkers declare that Purity is our very nature and that Fullness is our genuine reality. They said that we are never really "wanting." This was the lesson that Bharathiyas taught the world. This is the stream of spiritual strength that flowed from India and fertilised the world.

At the end of life, one should bring to the consciousness the great thoughts one has attained in life, the high feelings one entertained. This was the directive of the sages of India. They did not demand that one should bring to memory the faults and errors one committed in life. These are inevitable and universal. But the sages declare that one should be aware always of one's Reality and one should be engaged ever in contemplating its grandeur and glory. That, they said, is the greatest step to progress.

There is another fact that we have to pay attention to, more than all else. For Bharathiyas, religion means "experience" and nothing less. It is indeed pitiable that we very often forget this important fact. This secret must be imprinted on the heart of everyone. Only then can one be safe and secure. Not only this. It is not the way of thought of a Bharathiya to say that all things can be attained by self-exertion. The Bharathiya knows that Divine Will is the basis of everything. Religious principles have to be practised and their validity experienced. Listening to their exposition is of no use; learning some one set of arguments and conclusions and repeating them parrot-like are not enough. If they appeal to one's intellect and are approved by it as correct, that will not help at all. It must transform us. The reason why Bharathiyas posit God and declare that God is Being and Becoming is their experience, which is the highest proof. The declaration does not originate from the head, from the faculty of reason, the *yukti* (cleverness). The forefathers asserted that there is the entity, Atma, in each and that the Atma is but a spark of the Universal Atma, for they had become aware of it, deeply and without doubt. There were, in the past, thousands who had sought the experience and won it. Even today, such persons are not absent. In future too, they will be present. It is a thirst that affects man. Unless he contemplates God and confronts Him in bliss, unless he wins the awareness of the Atma that is his reality, man will be tormented by the thirst, the agony that he is "lacking completeness."

Man must first grasp the Truth. All religious factions and fights will vanish, as fast as man grasps the Reality. For, the name "follower of theistic code of morals," can be allotted only to one who has experienced God and realised His Glory. Only those who have realised Him in their hearts can have the bonds, that chain their hearts to the wheel of birth-death, broken. Mere platform orations do not indicate awareness of the Truth that has to be attained through religion.

Theistic faith is based on genuine experience. Once we accept this, self-examination starts and one is able to measure how far he has journeyed towards the goal or away from it. He will then realise that He is groping in the dark and dragging others into darkness to grope with him. Only then will men give up factional hatreds in the name of religious war on those professing different faiths. Those who revel in religious wars should be asked, "Have you seen God? Have you become aware of the Divine Atma? Or else, what authority have you to decry or deny this name of God? Are you, struggling in the darkness, attempting to draw me too into that darkness? Can a blind man lead another blind man along the road? That is an impossible task. Therefore, understand your Truth before you defame or deny mine."

✧ ✧ ✧ ✧ ✧

7. Be Yourself

He who has visualised the Atma principle that animates all can never condemn the religion of anyone. He will never enter any religious squabble or conflict. He will never talk lightly or demeaningly of another's faith. He will never disturb or despise the faith held by another. Only the ignorant with no spiritual experience, only those who do not know the depths of truth, will embark upon the condemnation of the faith of others. It is very unbecoming of man to indulge in or encourage religious conflicts, to ridicule the rites and ceremonies through which others adore God, and to label the religious practices of other people as "superstitions." For, each one has accepted the practice and holds on to it, since it confers Ananda on him!

The ONE is spoken of, by those who know, as MANY. The same thing is seen and experienced in different ways by different people, according to the angle of vision and the level of intelligence and awareness. Different persons describe the same thing or experience differently. How can anyone declare that they should not do so? Or that what they describe is wrong? No one has the right to disparage or deny.

Only those who strive to transcend the here and now and become aware of the Transcendent Principle of Godhead deserve the name Hindu. Those who revel in hurting others do not justify that name.

The inner core of Bharathiya culture is this realisation of the Unity of Atma principle that fills each heart with Universal Love. Those who are aware of this Unity and are well-established in it, are kith and kin of Bharathiyas, whichever country they may live in, whatever language is native to their tongues. Many human communities have, as the basis of their beliefs, the theory that man is a bundle of matter, and that this matter is subject to the laws of physics and chemistry. In the languages of the West, death is denoted as "the act of giving up life or Jiva," whereas in the language of Bharath, it is "giving up the body or the *Deha*." This is due to the faith of the Westerners that he is the body and the faith of the Bharathiya that he is not the body. The Bharathiyas assert and know that they have Atma as their Reality and that the Atma is enclosed in a body. The two views are widely disparate. A civilisation that is built on the shifting sand of worldly pleasure can last only for a little while. It will disappear from the surface of the earth. On the other hand, the civilisation of Bharath and of the countries that value and follow the civilisation of Bharath have survived for centuries and are vital even today. They show new and refreshing signs of more creative life. This fact has to be kept in mind by those Bharathiyas who have dedicated their lives to the imitation of other civilisations and cultures.

Imitation cannot build a stable culture. It can never become "civilisation." It is a sign of cowardice, not a quality that can ensure progress. It is the royal road to downfall. How can man draw inspiration for uplifting himself if he is engaged in hating himself and devaluing his achievements? The Bharathiya should feel no sense of shame when he brings back to memory his forefathers and the elders and teachers of the past who built the culture that nurtured him.

Instead, he ought to feel proud of his forefathers and the elders and teachers who shone among them. He must be proud that he has such persons as his ancestors, that his nation is of such holiness, and that his country is one that is endowed with such sacred characteristics. The children of Bharath have to fill themselves with the proud consciousness that in their native land were born wise persons who had attained the heights of self-realisation, as well as many others who had risen to peak of perfection.

Manifest the power that lies in self-exertion! Do not resort to the weak stratagem of imitating others. Instead absorb the good qualities that others may possess. We plant a seed in the soil. Then we supply it with the ingredients it needs—water, air, manure. The seed sprouts. It grows into a sapling. It becomes at last a huge tree. You will notice that it does not become either soil or manure, or air or water. These it makes use of, but it sticks to its own nature and grows into a tree.

May you too live like that tree. Of course we have much to learn from others. There is no need to doubt this fact. Those who refuse to learn thus, declare themselves fools. Whatever can promote your spiritual advance, you can learn from others. Imbibe them to the full, according to the lines laid down for your own progress in your own moral path or Dharma. *You* must live as *you,* not as someone else. Do not allow anyone to divert you away from your innate nature. Be immersed in your God, in your own imaginings and feelings, in the bliss that springs from your own heart, and in the delight derived from your sadhana (spiritual practice). When others try to prevent you from doing this, whatever plans they weave and whatever contrivances they employ, resist them at the cost of your own lives. Do not deny yourself that Divine Awareness and that Divine Ecstasy. This is the exhortation that echoes through the *Sathya Sai Vahini* of the Bharathiyas. Pull down the barriers that stand in the way and obstruct the free flow of the culture of this land that confers such sweetness and strength. Clear the channels through which it flows and cleanse them. Then it can follow its course, unimpeded.

Sai has willed that this country, Bharath, has to take this sadhana. For too long a time the theistic Dharma of this land has stopped moving. Its characteristic has been for a long time, static. Now it has to be made dynamic. It must vitalise the daily life of every human being. It must enter and fructify the palatial *Rajbhavan* (Royal palace) and the lowly hutments of the poorest in the land.

It is the treasure of everyone. Everyone has the right to inherit it and benefit by it. Having been born as man, one has a valid claim to share it. For this reason, Bharathiyas have to take it before every door and welcome everyone in each home to share it. As the air we breathe is, in God's creation, available to all, the Dharma of the awareness of God and His Power and Mercy has to be available to all. Bharathiyas must hold on to this wide outlook and the Universality and Unity of this message, the conflicts between desperate faiths and beliefs will disappear of themselves and peace and love will be restored on earth.

Imagine a house full of darkness since centuries. You may enter the house and pray to the darkness to leave the premises; or, you may shower abuse on it for days together; or, frighten it by threatening force. The darkness will stay, it cannot be diminished at all. It will not yield to your tactics. It cannot be scared out. But light a lamp, and it will flee that instant. The lamp of wisdom can save man from age-long darkness. This truth has to be well-recognised by man and, once recognised, he has to shape his life accordingly.

Man has an immensity in him. This is the core of Bharathiya thought. It is really a mystery how man came to regard himself as one condemned to fall! A person might strike us as demonic or as divine; in both the Atma is the Reality, to the same extent. You cannot say the Atma in one is less and in the other, is more. When faults are found in anyone, you will have to conclude that there are deficiencies in behaviour, that is all. Do not conclude that there is no Divine Atma in him. As a result of the company he keeps or the inefficiency of the society in which he grew, faults have grown in him. They are not native to his nature, which is Atmic. You will have to provide him good company and beneficial surroundings and persuade him to enter them. You should on no account condemn him as a born incorrigible, and keep him apart.

The body is composed of cells, which are made up of atoms. The atoms are also physical phenomena. They are fundamentally *jada*, or composite or unfeeling. The *Vedanthins* speak of a subtle body, separate from this gross body. That too is physical. It is the centre of subtle skills and force. It is in this body that all the subtle mental feelings and agitations take place. Every force can work only through some medium or other which is physical. The same power that operates the gross body works through the subtle processes of thought. They are not two different entities. One is the subtle form of the other, that is all.

What is the source of these powers? If we delve deep, we will find that there are two things in nature, *Akasa* (Sky element), and *Prana* (Life force). Akasa is the source of all the gross and subtle material one encounters; when Prana or Life-force contacts it, due to the impact, the Akasa principle transforms itself into either gross or subtle, in varying proportions. Prana too is omnipresent, like Akasa. It can also penetrate everywhere, and everything. Like the blocks of ice that water becomes and that float on water and that move about on water, the Prana acts on Akasa and bodies appear. Prana is the force that moulds the Akasa into various forms. The gross body is the vehicle of the Prana that it has shaped out of Akasa. The subtle body is of the form of thought, feeling, etc.

When the subtle body is transcended, the awareness of the Reality becomes manifest. Just as the nails on the fingers persist, however often we pare them, as part of our gross body, the subtle body too is an integral part of man's make-up.

✧ ✧ ✧ ✧ ✧

8. Bondage

A person can discard as many gross bodies in which he takes temporary residence, as the number of times he pares his nails. But the subtle body cannot be changed. It lasts and persists. This is the most secret doctrine of Bharathiya spiritual thought. Going further along this line of discovery, it can be revealed that man means: a complex of the gross body, the subtle body and the Jivi (the individual). The Vedantic philosophy would declare that the Jivi shares the quality of Eternal unchanging Everlastingness (*Nithya*). *Prakriti* or the objective world is also eternal, but with a difference. It undergoes perpetual change. It is never the same, but it persists forever. The basis for the objective world, namely, Prana (the life-force) and Akasa (space or ether) are eternal, but they act and interact without rest and manifest variously and manifoldly.

The Individual Atma (the Jivatma) did not have its origin in either Akasa or Prana. It is not material in nature. So it is eternal, without any change. It did not happen through the impact of Prana on Akasa, or Akasa on Prana. Things brought together will disintegrate. But things that are "themselves" ab initio cannot so come apart. For disintegration means "resuming the original nature," "becoming what it originally was," "reducing itself to its native substance." The gross body is the result of the combination of Prana and Akasa, and so it dissolves itself into its components. The subtle body too dissolves, but only after a long, long time. The Jivi is not brought together, so it cannot fall apart. It has no birth. It cannot be born. A unitive partless being can have no moment of origin.

The objective world or Prakriti, consisting of billions and billions of varied things, forces and events, is governed by the Will of God. God is All-knowing, All-penetrating, All-pervading. He is activating Prakriti and acting through Prakriti, all the time. Prakriti is ever in His care. His sovereignty is beginningless and endless. This is the doctrine of the dualists, the Dwaithins.

This gives room for one question. When the world is ruled by God, how does He permit it to be so wicked and vile? The answer given is that God is not responsible for the grief and the pain. The sins we commit are the progenitors of the grief we suffer. Joy and sorrow are the consequences of the good and the evil that man perpetrates. God is the

Witness. He does not punish, nor does He cause grief. The Jivi is beginningless, that is to say, he has no birth; but he involves himself in incessant activity and so he has to go through the inevitable consequences of that activity. This is the experience of everyone, the characteristic of everyone's mind. This is the unbreakable law of the objective world or Prakriti. Grief or joy is the image of the activity one engages in. It is the resound, the reflection, the reaction. The Jivi *can* be the witness without concerning himself with the good and the bad of the activity. When involvement happens, good will have to be experienced when good is done, and evil will have to be experienced when evil is done.

The Vedantha asserts that the Jivi is by its very nature, pure and unblemished. This is the accepted doctrine according to Bharathiya thought. But this truth has been befogged by ignorance and neglect. So, maya pollutes the experience and the shade of ignorance breeds evil. But when *sathkarma* or beneficial activity is engaged in, the clouds of maya are scattered and the Reality of the Self is realised. All beings, all jivis are, by their very nature, pure. Good acts can remove the taints of evil deeds and preserve its essential purity. Then, the Jivi is led into the God- ward path, the *Devayana*. The Godward urge will transform the words, the thoughts and the deeds of the individual.

We cannot think without words. Words are the essential material for thought. When the individual drops the body, the words enter the mind; the mind enters the prana or life-force and the prana merges in the Atma. The Atma (individualised in the body) when it liberates itself rushes to the *Surya Loka*, the Region of the Solar Principle, the Surya. From thence, it reaches the region of Brahma, the *Brahma Loka*. Having reached that region, the individualised Atma or Jivatma has no more concern with Prakriti. It will exist there till and end of Time. It will experience boundless Delight. It will have all powers except the powers of Creation.

The authority to rule over the Cosmos is exclusive to God. God is free from desires of all varieties. Man's duty is but to offer Him Love and worship Him through Love. This raises man to the highest status among beings. Those who are unaware of this status or incapable of discharging its responsibilities belong to other categories. They too offer and worship, they too engage themselves in beneficial activity. But they crave for the fruits they hope to gain. They perform acts motivated by a desire to benefit from the results that emerge therefrom. "We have helped the helpless; so, our path will be smooth and safe. We have uplifted the downtrodden; so, we can avoid troubles on our road. We have busied ourselves in singing the Lord's Glory in chorus (Bhajan); so, we are sure of Heaven"—these are the calculations of people of this nature who engage themselves in "good acts." When such people give up their bodies, that is to say, when such people die, their words will merge in their minds, their minds will merge in their Prana, and the Prana, thereafter will merge in the Jivi, and the Jivatma will travel to the Region of the Moon Principle (the *Chandra*

Loka), that is to say, the Loka of the Presiding Deity of the Mind…suggesting that they have to enter again the realm of the mind with all its agitations and turmoils of wants and wishes. In the Chandra Loka, such Jivis will experience some satisfaction and delight, as long as the consequence of the good acts lasts. That is why it is said in the scriptures: *Ksheene Punye, marthya-lokam visanthi*. (When the acquired merit is spent, they enter again the world of mortal men). The Jivatma encases itself in a body equipped with sense organs, etc. appropriate to the earned consequences of the deeds of the previous body, and starts another life-career. The residence of the soul in the Chandra Loka is what the Hindus refer to as the time spent as a Deva in Heaven or as an Angel according to Christian and Islamic religions. The name Devendra given to the Lord of these Devas is an indication of a position of authority. Thousands have risen to that position.

According to the Vedas, when the highest good is observed, that person is elevated to the position of Devendrahood. The soul raised previously to that position will descend to the earth and resume its career in human form. Just as on earth monarchs change, in heaven too rulers cannot escape rise and fall. The residents of Heaven too are subject to the law of ups and downs. It is only the Brahma Loka that is free from birth and death, rise and fall, ups and downs. This is the basic doctrine of Bharathiya thought, its eternal nectar, administered to humanity.

When the Jivatma is as a Deva in the Chandra Loka, it cannot manifest any Karma. Only man can express himself through Karma which binds him by its consequence. Karma means activity undertaken with desire, with an eye on the result. When the soul is in Chandra Loka as a Deva, it is content and satisfied and so, it will not crave for activity for earning pleasure or achieving some success. The residence in that Loka is the reward it has secured for the good deeds done by it in the past, or it may be the prize won for such goodness. When the delight emanating from the good deeds is experienced and spent away, the balance of the consequence accumulated has to be suffered, and so the soul has to come as man on earth. Then, attaining the highest good and engaging himself in acts of highest potency for merit, he can cleanse his heart and reach Brahma Loka from whence there is no coming back.

The word *Naraka* (Hell) can nowhere be found in the Vedas. The conception of Hell is foreign to the spiritual thought of Bharathiyas. The idea of Hell and the various descriptions of Hell are all later additions in the Sastras and Puranas. The authors of these texts believed that religion will be incomplete if it does not posit Hell. They laid down diverse tortures as part of Hell, but they laid down one limit to the pain Hell inflicts. They declared that there can be no death in Hell. The purpose for which Hell was created was only to incite fear among the people in order to make them desist from sin.

But *Adwaitha* does not posit Heaven or Hell. It is concerned only with Bondage and Liberation, Ignorance and Illumination. It is known as Vedantha. There is no faith higher than what Vedantha stands for.

✧ ✧ ✧ ✧ ✧

9. One With The One

The Jagat or Cosmos was created by God out of Himself, so that He is the originator as well as the material of the Cosmos. As a result, He is Full (Paripoorna). The Creation is also Full and the Individual Atma is also Full. Therefore, many full entities are postulated. God made the Cosmos manifest from Himself, when this declaration is made, the doubt may naturally arise, "How could God become these walls, these tables?" God is supremely pure, how could He become these impure things? This is another doubt that is uppermost to some.

Let us seek the answers. Man is fundamentally Atma, but he has the encasement of a body, hasn't he? From one point of view, man is not distinct from the body, is he? In spite of this, however, man feels that he is not this body, that his reality is distinct from it, that he is not the baby he was or the old man he is, that he is neither male nor female, and that he persists through babyhood, boyhood, middle age and old age, masculinity and femininity and all the other stages and changes. So too, the Cosmos and all creation are but the billion bodies of God. He is all this and in all this, but He is changeless and eternal. Nature is amenable to change. The Atma too can contract or expand, blossom or fade, shine or be befogged. Bad deeds will diminish its splendour by clouding its brilliance. Its innate and genuine truth and wisdom may be hidden by evil thoughts and deeds. Those acts and practices that can disclose the native splendour and glory of the Atman are termed "good."

The Atma is "unbound" at first, but later it is seen as limited and restricted. Through good deeds and activities, it resumes its vastness and boundlessness. Everyone without any difference has the opportunity to achieve this transformation. When the time gets ripe, everyone can succeed in this and liberate himself from the bounds and bonds. But the Jagat (Cosmos) will not end. That is eternal, incapable of being destroyed. This is the explanation of the second school of philosophy in India. The first one is the dualist or the Dwaitha. The second one is the *Visishtadwaitha* or the Special Adwaitha. This is a higher stage in spiritual inquiry and experience. It posits three entities—God, the Atma, and Nature, and speaks of an integration of the three. The dualists posit that the Cosmos is a vast machine designed and operated by God. The Visishtadwaithins declare that it is a phenomenon that is interpenetrated and imbued with the Divine. But the Adwaithins or the non-dualists assert that God is not outside the Cosmos, that He became the Cosmos (Jagat), and that He is all that is. There is nothing except God, no Other, no Second. This truth has to be accepted by all. This is the highest Truth. To say that God is the Atma and the Cosmos is as the Body which He operates and lives in, is not correct. To assert that the Atma (God) is eternal and changeless but the Cosmos which is His Body can be subject to change and transformation is also not satisfying.

What does it signify when it is said, "God is the *Upadanakarana*, the Proximate Cause of the Cosmos"? Proximate cause means the cause which produced the effect. The "effect" is the "cause" in another form. It cannot be separate from the cause. Every effect that we notice is but the cause that has assumed a new form. The Cosmos is the effect, God is the Cause—these statements only stress the fact that the Cosmos is but God in another form. When it is argued that the body is limited and subtle, and that It leads one to the Cause, that is, God, or it was from God that it has evolved and taken shape, the non-dualists would reply that it was God Himself who manifested in the form of the Cosmos.

It may be doubted whether all this multiplicity of things and beings are really God. Yes. It is the Truth. All these that the senses cognise, that come into the awareness, are God. There is nothing else but He. Our bodies, minds, intellects, consciousness—all *are* God.

Here, another doubt may arise. Why should God be so many individualised beings? Why should He be so many Jivatmas? Will God, who is of one Form, manifest Himself as so many? How did this happen? If God has transformed Himself into the Cosmos, He should have subjected Himself to change; all things in Nature that are by their very composition subject to change, suffer both birth and death. And if God has come within the precincts of change, does it mean that He too has to die someday? Has he to undergo change and ultimately end? Keep in mind this point also. Then, there is another point to be considered. How much of God, what portion of God became the Cosmos?

The Adwaithins say, "Whatever the portion you may allot, or guess about, remember this: The Cosmos does not exist. It is an illusion. It never is, has been or will be. The Creation of the Cosmos, the dissolution of the Cosmos, these billions of individuals emerging and merging, all this is but a dream. There is no individualised Jivatma at all, no separated Atma. How can there be billions of Jivatmas? There is only ONE Indivisible Complete Absolute. Like the one sun reflected as a billion suns in a billion lakes, ponds, and drops of water, the Jivatmas are but reflections of the One in the minds that it shines upon. This is what Bharathiya thought emphasises most clearly through the Adwaithin thinkers. Those who cannot grasp this truth are under the influence of Maya or delusion, it can be said.

Dreams too have to be based on reality. Without a basic reality, the "dependent idea or fact" cannot exist.

Without a basic thing, subsequent things cannot emanate. Without a basic being, subsequent beings cannot manifest. That base is God or Easwara. He is Full. He is the Mind, the Body, the Atma. You are only as real as a dream. For the eye that can see reality, the Cosmos is, not this multiplicity of name and form, but mere *Sath-Chith-Ananda*, Being-Awareness-Bliss. Just think of your dream. It does not arise from somewhere outside you nor do the varied images and activities disappear into some place outside you. They arise in you and disappear into you. While dreaming, you consider the events and persons as real, and you experience, as really as in the waking stage, the feelings of grief, delight, fear, anxiety, and joy. You do not dismiss them at the time as illusory. The Cosmos is the dream of God. It arises in Him and merges in Him. It is the product of His Mind. These lives and repeated arrivals, all are the fanciful weavings of Maya, unreal fantasies, illusory agitations, unreal appearances. You are the Full, you are God. God is You. Those who have experienced this highest wisdom can attain oneness with the ONE, here and now.

✧ ✧ ✧ ✧ ✧

10. The Yogis

There are three steps in the progression of philosophic inquiry (or Vedantic thought) in India. They are the Adwaithic and Visishtadwaithic and the Dwaithic. It is not possible to advance beyond these three steps by any human endeavour. Adwaithic thought is beyond reach of the common man. It is not so easily comprehensible. To conceive it with the intellect is itself hard. To experience it, a powerful faculty of penetration is needed. Therefore, it is best to start with the dualist or Dwaithic step, and experience it as the reality behind things. Then, the second stage of Visishtadwaitha is rendered easier to reach.

The individual must progress as fast or as steadily as the community. We pass through boyhood, childhood, adolescence, youth, middle age and old age. It is an imperceptible but inevitable progress. We experience each only when we are passing through it. So too, with these three stages of philosophic discovery. Each of these views is latent in the rest and each proceeds out of the experience of the previous stage. It is not possible to be aware of all three at the same time. Based on our sadhana and the experiences gained therefrom, each of these viewpoints comes into the consciousness and forms the spring of action and thought.

Those who assert that the Universe is real, but declare at the same time that the existence of God is but a dream, are only proving themselves foolish. For when the effect, namely, the Cosmos is real, it must have a Cause, for how can there be an effect with no cause? God can be denied only when the Universe is denied. God can disappear, only when the Cosmos disappears. What now appears as the Cosmos is really God. This is the vision that the true Sadhaka will get when he succeeds in his endeavour. As a matter of fact, the Universe we experience is the dream. When we awake from the dream, the Truth of its being God will shine in the consciousness. From the beginning of time, the God whom we posit outside ourselves has been the reality inside us also. This Truth too will become steady in the faith of man.

Of course, there is no philosophy existent that can be satisfying to all types and levels of mental equipment. Each has a distinct value. The stages of intellectual development, or the powers of reasoning are different from each other.

So, the three schools of philosophical interpretation mentioned above (the Dwaithic, the Visishtadwaithic and the Adwaithic) attain acceptance among different temperaments and different groups of people. Therefore, no one school has the right to claim superiority and impute inferiority. Only those who are unwise will resort to such tactics.

When people approach us with fanatic views, we must meet them with a smile, eager and yearning, filled with devotion to God. One can get intoxicated, of course; but only as a result of quaffing the wine of *Prema* (love). When someone who is fanatic for work approaches us we must share with him our skill and strength and join with him in work. By this means, it is possible to bring harmony between followers of various faiths and philosophic thoughts. It will bring together schools of thought and belief. If only this principle of harmony and harmonious co-operation had become a permanent asset of each man, how excellent it would be? How happy the world would have been if everyone had this knowledge that his viewpoint can at best be only partial and that it requires the harmonious commingling of many other facets to posit Truth?

Yoga means "coming together." In India, where yoga is flowing in the veins of everyone since ages, it is possible to have the harmonious coexistence of many faiths and beliefs, which is the ideal type of Universal Religion. Those who can heroically put their faith into daily living can accomplish this "togetherness" in the human community. Togetherness or Union can be established between one's outer behaviour and inner nature. The Sadhaka (aspirant for spiritual progress), intent on the path of Prema, can strive for Union between himself and the embodiment of Prema, namely, God. The Vedantin can achieve the Union of all that IS in the one concept of God. The path of Yoga is designated differently in Sanskrit under different contexts, but those who are able to conceive and execute the Union are revered as Yogis.

Those who strive through activities and achievements to establish the Union are the Karma yogis. Those who follow the Prema path, are the Bhakthi yogis. Those who strive to manifest their latent powers and canalise them are the Raja yogis. Those who stick to logical analysis and rational interpretations and attain intuitive perception are the Jnana Yogis. In the Bharathiya spiritual history, these four types recur again and again.

First, the Karma yogi. He adopts the path of establishing union with Godhead by elevating and sublimating acts. We meet in the world many who seem to have been born, just to accomplish one particular mission or project. Their intellect is not satisfied with mere imagination or planning. Their minds will be full of actual concrete achievements which they yearn to realise. For such people, a guidebook or Sastra is needed to direct them along beneficial paths. Everyone in the world is seen engaged in some activity or other, all the time. Yet, very few know the significance and worthwhileness of Karma; or, how best to realise the best results out of this inescapable trait. Hence, life is being made banal and barren. Karma Yoga teaches man the awareness of this significance and guides him along to achieve the maximum benefit out of the activity. Where, when and how Karma has to be done, how spiritual urges can reinforce strength of mind in the performance of Karma, and how Karma is to be taken up so that spiritual development can result—these are taught us by the Karma Yoga.

There is one great objection raised by some people about this and we have to pay some attention to it. The objection is that Karma Yoga involves too much physical strain. But basically, it is the company that one keeps that decides the strain and the stress that the mind and the body of man are subjected to. "I like very much to engage myself in only this task." "I sought only to do good to him, but he ignored my desire and tried to injure me," these are the usual causes for the strain and stress mentioned above. Such disappointment makes one lose interest in activity. It wants to do good and It seeks to do good to someone in some way, hoping to derive joy therefrom and distribute joy. When such joy does not arise, despair sets in.

But without getting attached, without being aware as to whom the Karma helps or how, the lesson that Karma Yoga teaches is—do the Karma, as Karma, for the sake of the Karma. Why does the Karma yogi fill his hands with work? That is his real nature. He feels that he is happy, while doing work. That is all. He does not bargain for results. He is not urged by any calculation. He gives, but never receives. He knows no grief, no disappointment; for he has not hoped for any benefit.

The second Path: Bhakthi Yoga. This is congenial for those who are emotionally-oriented. It is the path for those capable of filling their hearts with Love. The urge is to have God as the Beloved. His activities will be different, for they relate to incense-burning, gathering flowers for worship, building shrines and temples where he could install and adore symbols of Beauty, Wisdom and Power.

Are you inclined to remark that this is not the right means of achieving union with Divinity? Remember that saints and sages, great spiritual leaders and guides throughout the world have emerged just from this devotional and dedicatory stage of spiritual endeavour. Some faiths tried to imagine God as formless, and described worship of God through such various acts as blasphemy, tried to suppress the Bhakthi cults and in the process, they slighted the Reality and Its Power and Majesty. The belief that God cannot be symbolised in a Form is evidence of blindness. The charge that such worship is barren is a hollow charge. The history of the world is the witness to the efficacy of Bhakthi. It is not proper to ridicule these activities, ceremonials and rituals and the descriptions of the lives of sadhakas who adhered to them in order to earn Union with

Divinity. Let those who yearn after the joy of worshipping the Form do so. Certainly, it will be a sin to shatter their faith and treat it as infructuous.

The glory of the great heroes of the spirit, those who have scaled the highest peaks of Realisation, and those who attain spiritual fulfilment is exercising immense influence on the mind of mankind. It is as a result of a long line of such seers that the spiritual message of India has attracted the attention of all nations. If India has been able to earn the reverence of the world, the reason has to be sought in the precious treasure that they have earned and preserved. Here, love of God and fear of sin have been the chief pillars of life and the everlasting guides for living. Bharath has won a name for being a holy land, a land steeped in renunciation and in spiritual sadhanas aimed at union with the Absolute, renowned for *tyaga* (renunciation, detachment) and yoga. The urges that this culture encouraged were all directed to the conquest of the vagaries of the mind.

Can the explanations offered by this culture on the nature and characteristics of Reality be palatable to those afflicted by agitated feelings and passion? To the great builders of this culture, God was tangible Truth, the one and Only Real Fact, the Goal of their entire Love. So the inheritors and followers of this culture treat the nihilist arguments based on the inescapably limited "reason" as the fool is treated in the story. The fool saw an idol, and eager to discover the God he broke it to pieces with a hammer!

The Bhakthi Yoga will teach such people the path of Love. It will tell them not to love with a view to gain profit. Love all, love all as you love yourselves. No harm can come to you then. It will only spread joy and happiness to all. God is present in all beings as love. So the Love is directed to and accepted by, not the individual but by God who is resident there. The seeker of God who relies on the path of devotion and dedication soon becomes aware of this fact.

Some love God as the Mother, some others as the Father, and some love God as "dearest and closest Friend." There are others who regard God as the Beloved, the only desired Goal. They all endeavour to merge their Love with the Ocean of Love that God is. Wherever Love is evident, take it that it is God's own Love. God is the greatest Lover of mankind. Therefore, when anyone decides to serve man whom He loves, God showers Grace in plenty. When the human heart melts at the suffering of others and expands as a result of that sympathy, believe that God is present there. That is the sign of the validity of the path of devotion, the Bhakthi Yoga.

Now, about *Raja Yoga*: Raja Yoga means the process of establishing mastery over the mind. One need not surrender one's intellect or follow the guidelines of religious leaders. There is no chance of being misled or mistaken. At every step, one has to rely on one's own intellect and experience, as tested by oneself.

Every being has three varieties of instruments for acquiring knowledge, and through that knowledge, wisdom. The first is "instinctive"; this is very strong, active and advanced in animals. This is the earliest, the lowest and therefore, the least beneficial of the three. The second is the "rational," the instrument that seeks the cause and the effect thereof. This is most evident in man. The instinct can operate only in the limited field of senses and sensory experiences. In man the instinctive knowledge is largely subordinated by the rational instruments. The limits of the rational are very thin; reason can range over vastly wider fields. In spite of this, reason too is capable of very poor performance only. Its reach is restricted. It can proceed only a certain distance. It cannot venture further. The road that logic takes is not straight. It is more circular, returning again and again, to the place from which it started.

Take for example, our knowledge of the objective world, of the elements and energies that compose it. That which urges and prompts the objective world and its components does not stop with just this much. It absorbs also that which is immanent outside the objective world. And so, the extent that reason can spread over and explain is as the "consciousness" that is imprisoned in the tiny molecule, as compared with the vastness and grandeur of the transcendent fullness.

For us to go across the boundaries of reason into this full, free realm of intuition, certain spiritual exercises and disciplines are essential. They can be grouped under the name, God-propelled Jnana (the highest wisdom). For, we have only three stages of Jnana—*Sahajajnana* (Native, derived from the senses of action and perception). *Yukti-yuktajnana* (Knowledge derived by the process of discrimination and evaluation), and *Easwaraprerithajnana* (God-induced knowledge gained through Grace by inner vision or intuition). The first of these is the knowledge possessed by animals. The second is the characteristic of man, and the third is the special treasure of high-souled individuals. It is possible for everyone to foster, cultivate and develop the seedlings of this third Jnana. For, the capacity is latent in all.

Another fact also has to be borne in mind. The three are stages of growth and so not three mutually exclusive types of knowledge. The *Easwarapreritha-jnana* will not contradict the yukti-yuktajnana. It will only bring to light what is unmanifest in the *yukti-yuktajnana*. The later stage only confirms and elaborates the previous ones. Afflicted by the vagaries of the mind and its fancies, some take their distorted attitudes as God given or Grace-induced. And they may even call upon others to heed their counsel. They lead men astray by their barren guidance. These morons announce that their absurd prattle is God-propelled.

True teaching can never be counter to the yukti-yuktajnana, the conclusion arrived at by discrimination and evaluation. The Yogas mentioned above are all established in consonance with this view. Raja Yoga has to be practised mostly by the mind and its resolution. This is a vast subject and so, we shall consider here only its central theme. It is something that is the only refuge for the lowest of the low and the highest of the Yogis—namely, single-pointed meditation. For the person engaged in research in a laboratory, for one walking along a road, or for a scholar reading a book, or an individual writing a letter, or driving a car, the concentration of all their attention on the articles before them and the activity they are engaged in is very important. He understand the nature and peculiarities of the object he is handling. The more intense your concentration, the more successful will be your activity. When the mental abilities are focused on one effort, knowledge can be acquired quicker and from a wider field. And that is the only way by which knowledge can be earned.

Concentration will enable one, whoever he is, whatever the activity he is engaged in, to finish it much better than otherwise. Whether in material assignments, or in ordinary day-to-day work or in spiritual sadhana, concentration of mental energies is a must if success is to be achieved. It is the key that can open the treasure chest of Jnana. This is the most important aspect of Raja Yoga. It can even be said that it is the only important aspect of that Yoga. Millions of unwelcome, unwanted, unnecessary and even harmful thoughts enter our minds and confound their activities. These have to be kept out. The mind has to be guarded and controlled and kept under our rigorous supervision. Raja

Yoga is the one refuge for persons endeavouring to win this victory.

Jnana Yoga is mostly devoted to the study of principles, basic principles. This Universe or Cosmos that we cognise as outside ourselves can be explained by means of various theories of knowledge, but no one of them can be convincing to the uninitiated. The Jnana Yogi weaves many such theories and hypotheses. He is not convinced of the reality of any material object in the Universe, or of any activity or even of anyone else who propounds any other explanation. He believes that he should transcend the daily chores of life and not be bound by social or other obligations. In the vast Ocean of ISNESS, or *Sath* (Truth, reality), all objects are but drops, in his view. They are all struggling to move from the circumference to the Centre, from which they manifested through Maya. The Jnana Yogi too yearns to merge in the Centre, the Core of Reality, away from the tangle of apparent diversity. He exerts himself to *become* the Truth, not only to become aware of It. Of course, as soon as he is aware of It, he becomes IT. He cannot tolerate the thought that he and Truth are separate and distinct.

The Divine is his only kith and kin. He knows none other. He does not entertain any other urge, any other attachment, any other desire. God is all in all. He cannot be affected by grief or joy, failure or success. He sees and experiences only one unbroken, unchallenged stream of bliss-consciousness. For the person who is firmly established in this state, the world and its ups and downs appear trivial and illusory. In order to stay in that Consciousness, he has to counter the pulls of the senses and face the fascinations of the world without any agitation of mind.

The Jnana Yogi is vigilant against the temptations held before him by his senses, and turning them aside, he approaches the Divine and seeks strength and solace there. He realises that the power and energy that vitalise the tiniest of the tiny and the vastest of the vast is the same Divine Principle. His actions, thoughts, and words reveal this vision he has experienced. This is the *Paramartha Drishti*, the Supravision. It sees all elements—the earth, fire, water, wind and sky—as the Divine itself and all beings—man, beast, bird, and worm—as emanations from God and therefore fully Divine.

One fact has to be noted here. If a person has this knowledge of the immanence of the Divine, and even of its transcendence, he cannot be honoured as a *Jnani* (wise, liberated person). For, the knowledge has to be digested through actual experience. This is the crucial test. It is not enough if the intellect nods approval and is able to prove that Godhead is all. The belief must penetrate and prompt every moment of living and every act of the believer. Jnana should not be merely a bundle of thoughts or a packet of neatly constructed principles. The faith must enliven and enthuse every thought, word and deed. The self must be soaked in the nectar of the Jnana.

The intellect is a poor instrument. For, what the intellect approves as correct today is tomorrow rejected by the same intellect on second thoughts! Intellect cannot judge things finally and for all time. Therefore, seek for the experience. Once that is won, the Atman can be understood "as all this." That is the Jnana Yoga. According to the Bharathiya way of thought, the Vedas are taken as the Voice of God. Thus, the Vedas are the primary source of all knowledge for Bharathiyas. Everything is tested on the basis of Vedas. The ancient sages have laid down that what agrees with the Vedas is agreeable to man; what does not thus agree cannot agree with him. The Vedas were not spoken by humans, or composed by men and women. They were heard and recorded by sages, and transmitted by the guru to the pupil for generations by word of mouth. The guru recited, the pupil listened and recited just as the guru did, with the same care and correctitude. Thus the Vedas have been handed down for centuries. No one can determine the exact date when the Vedas were first heard or recited. Therefore, they are taken as *Sanathana* or Eternal.

At this point, we have to keep in mind another very important truth. All other religions prevalent in the world hold as authoritative communications made to some holy person by God Himself in His Corporate Form, or through some Superhuman personalities or embodiments of parts or portions of Divinity. Bharathiyas do not follow this line. They declare that the Vedas are based on no human authority. They do not depend on any man for their validity.

They are emanations direct from God. They are primeval. They are their own authority and validity. They were not written down or composed, constructed or put together.

The Cosmos or Creation is limitless, eternal and it has neither beginning nor end. So too, the Voice of God, namely the Vedas have no limit, they are eternal, they have no beginning nor end. "*Vid*," the root from which the word Veda is derived, means, "to know." When Knowledge began the Vedas too manifested. The Rishis visualised and announced them. They are the "seers of *manthras*"—the *manthra-drishtas*.

The Vedas have two major sections: the Karma Kanda and the Jnana Kanda. First comes the Karma Kanda and it is followed by the Jnana Kanda. In the Karma Kanda, a number of different "*krathus*" or sacrifices in which oblations are offered in the sanctified fire are mentioned. Most of them have been given up by Bharathiyas in recent times, since it has become difficult to perform them with the exactitude the Vedic rules prescribe. Some still continue in a very attenuated form. In the Karma Kanda, the moral codes are insisted upon very much. The moral rules and restrictions regulating life and conduct refer to the *Brahmachari* (the student) stage, the *Grihastha* (householder) stage, the *Vanaprastha* (recluse) stage and the *Sanyasa* (monastic) stage. Also, the Karma Kanda declares what is right and wrong for people following various professions and occupying different statuses. These are being followed here and there, in some thin form, by people in India.

The Jnana Kanda is called Vedantha or the end of the Vedas, the Goal, the Finale. The Jnana Kanda is enshrined in the Upanishads. The adherents of the Dwaitha, Visishtadwaitha and Adwaitha schools of philosophical thought, the worshippers of Shiva, Vishnu, Sakthi, Surya and Ganapathi—all accept the supreme authority of the Vedas. They may interpret the Upanishads and other texts according to their own predilections and intellectual calibre, but no one dare question the authority of the Veda or the Vedantha. So, it is possible to use the words Hindu, Bharathiya or Vedantin, to the same person. The various schools of philosophical thought current at the present time may appear difficult to comprehend or as derived from unripe understanding; but when the matter is thought over in quiet, or the texts are studied in silence, or investigated without prejudice it will become clear that they have all relied on the points raised and the conclusions arrived at in the Upanishads. The Upanishads are being symbolised and worshipped in image form in temples and in private shrines, as a tribute to this universal appeal. They have entwined themselves, inseparably, in our lives.

The Vedas are "endless": *Anantho vai vedaah*. But they were reduced into four collations and their essence was preserved in those forms. For promoting peace and prosperity in the world, the four were then taught and propagated. They are the *Rig, Sama, Yajur* and *Atharvana Vedas*. They uphold Dharma (Righteousness), proclaim the Reality, and promote peace and harmony by developing among men the attitudes of worship, music, and adoration and also by the cultivation of skill in weaponry and war. They present the ideal before mankind, and exhort them to follow.

Whether the Bharathiya is aware of it or not, invariably, every right act of his, will have some Vedic injunction or prohibition behind it as the regulator or the illuminator. From marriage rites until funeral rites and even the rites for the propitiation of the *manes* (ancestors), the Vedas are the guides. A true Bharathiya should never forget the Vedas or be ungrateful to them. The dualists, the special-monists, the monists—all direct their lives according to lines laid down in the past by the sages. But they do not now know the origin and the purpose of these guidelines. If only they do, the fruit will be much more plentiful and permanent.

✧ ✧ ✧ ✧ ✧

11. Value In Vedas

"*Vetthi ithi Vedah*"; Knowing, knowledge is Veda. That is to say, man can know from the Vedas, the Code of Right Activity and the Body of Right Knowledge. The Vedas teach man his duties from birth to death. They describe his rights and duties, obligations and responsibilities in all stages of life—as a student, householder, recluse and monk. In order to make plain the Vedic dicta and axioms and enable all to understand the meaning and purpose of the do's and don'ts, the Vedangas, Puranas and Epic texts appeared, in course of time. Therefore, if man is eager to grasp his own significance and true reality, he has to understand the importance of these later explanatory compositions also.

This is the reason why the ancients taught the Vedangas and other related texts even before the pupils learnt the Vedas. This was a must in the *Gurukulas* or Hermitage

Schools of the past. In those days, the Bharathiyas studied the "Fourteen *Vidyas*" or "Subjects." The Vedas were learnt by rote. The master of the Vedas, who had learnt the Vedas in this manner was called Jada, or Inert. But the word did not convey the meaning that he had not known anything. It only meant that he had nothing more to learn and was therefore "inactive" and "content." Through the study of the Vedas, he had become the master of all knowledge. In order to make this human career worthwhile, the study of the Vedas was considered very essential.

The stream of Indian culture always emphasised the authority of the Vedas as the supreme authority for deciding the values of human living. Of the Vedas, the first is the Rig Veda. It is generally considered as composed of ten "*mandalas*" or sections. In the first nine sections, hymns in praise of God under the names of Agni, Indra, Marut, Ushas, etc., are found. Historians and researchers have suggested certain theories to explain how these hymns of praise arose. Men in those days realised that *Agni* (Fire), *Vayu* (Air), *Marut* (Wind), etc. were far more powerful than they; and so they described their Divine qualities and propitiated them.

The second of the Vedas is the Yajur Veda. This Veda has two recensions—the Krishna Yajur Veda and the Sukla Yajur Veda. This Veda refers to the Ganga river and its region. It is the source of the Uttara Mimamsa school of thought and interpretation. The people had by then demarcated the forest areas from the cultivable areas around the villages and had taken to habitation in the villages. There is a prominent reason that prompted the separation of certain portions of the Veda into the Yajur Veda. The Yajur Veda has seven sections called *Aranyakas* or Forest Texts, indicating by that very name, that it refers more to disciplines and spiritual exercises which can be practised only in the seclusion and silence of the forest.

The third Veda is the Sama Veda. In this collection, many of the hymns (Rks) of the Rig Veda are repeated, but with additional musical notes so that they may be sung during Vedic rituals and ceremonies. So the Sama Veda is mainly *Swara* or musical notation. The Rig-Veda Aryans lived on the banks of the Sindhu river while the Yajur-Veda people came to their awareness when they were on the banks of the Ganga. The Sama Veda songs are also visualisations of the same era, but the people seem to have occupied even the middle region of Bharath. The Sama Veda is referred to as the Gaana Veda also, in order to highlight its musical nature. All musical schools are derivatives from the styles that are marked out by the Sama Veda. All tones and notes are embedded in that Veda.

The fourth is the Atharvan or Atharva Veda. Many have described it in many diverse ways. Some have even denied it the status of a Veda. Others say that it is made up of what remained after the collation of the rest. In the other Vedas, the might and mystery of the Gods are described.

But in this Veda, the possibility of man acquiring certain powers and mysteries by his own effort and exercises are mentioned. This is its specialty. Hatha Yoga, Thiraskarani Vidya, Ashta Yoga—these are made available for man only in this Veda. Of course, by winning the Grace of God, man can acquire even skills that are otherwise impossible of attainment.

In short, it must be realised that the Vedas are very important for man and that they cover the entire range of knowledge. They are the source and spring of Bharathiya culture. They are the recordings of visions and divine experiences. Their source is not some one definite person. They were revealed by God Himself, of His own innate mercy. The Vedic inheritance has been preserved pure and unsullied even to this day, because, it was handed down from the master to the disciple, in regular succession. Since it is timeless and authorless, it is worthy of acceptance by all. No one can afford to neglect or deny their value.

Whatever may be the diversities in contents, the commentators agree that the essential teaching of all the four Vedas is the same. The sections dealing with rites, modes of worship and the conclusions of inquiry help man to achieve the four goals of life—Dharma, *Artha* (wealth), *Kama* (desire for things of sensory world) and Moksha. Since it is very hard to master the Vedas, we have developed a vast Smrithi literature to expound the Sruthi texts—the

Puranas and the Ithihasas. Farsighted seers composed these out of historical and legendary incidents and events.

Karma and Jnana are related as cause and effect, and so, the Karma sections of the Sruthi and Smrithi, which emphasised activity led to the discovery of new facets of Truth and rendered the ideas of a transcendent God clearer and nearer. So too, the discovery of clearer concepts of God through spiritual inquiry along the Jnana *Marga* (path) fed "activity" with better meaning and higher purpose. The benefit of Karma was proportionate to the faith and the faith in Karma was in proportion to the awareness of God, won through Jnana. For involving oneself in good activities, Jnana is an essential prerequisite. That Jnana has ultimately to be derived from the Vedas. It is based on the teachings of the Vedas.

Karma is, really speaking, the practice of Dharma. The Upanishads give us guidance on what has to be done and what has to be avoided, in the spiritual journey. They direct us to revere the mother as God, revere the father as God, revere the preceptor as God, revere the guest as God and also, warn us that Truth shall not be neglected, Dharma shall not be neglected. So, there are both positive and negative instructions—follow these counsels not others. Whatever conduces to your progress in goodness, accept; avoid other counsels—thus do the Upanishads instruct.

In those centuries, the King himself studied in hermitages at the feet of the Upanishadic sages, and helped others to study by granting economic aid profusely to the centres of learning which shone as repositories of Vedic lore. As the king, so the subjects. Fostering the Vedas meant fostering the Vedic scholars and practitioners, the Vedavidis. At the present time, encouragement is afforded and scholarship is honoured in other branches of learning. The Vedic scholars are not given similar encouragement and emoluments. But this is an important aspect that has to be attended to.

Dharmo rakshati rakshitah; Dharma protects those who protect it, says the Sruthi. If people come forward to foster the sources of Dharma, that good act, by itself, will help foster those who do it. The study of the Vedas has become today the task of the economically weak. People have reconciled themselves to this situation. They associate the study with such a sad and pitiable picture. Vedic studies have come down to this deplorable pass. The very pundits who have attained scholarship in the Vedas are using it as a commercial item that can be sold. They do not demonstrate the value of Vedic study in the peace and harmony of their lives and thus win reverence for the Vedas by personal example. The Vedas are being misused by them for earning a pittance, rather than liberation and peace. This is the reason why Dharma is receiving a setback and anxiety and fear are spreading among men. The World can win back peace and harmony only when such persons are persuaded to practise the ideals laid down in the Vedas, and thereby serve as beacon lights to guide mankind aright. Else, downfall is inevitable.

The Bharathiya spiritual stream has until the present times fertilised Vedic learning and practice. Its message has been always, "Journey forward along the Vedic Path." One may dilate on Vedantha and Vedas; but unless one holds forth the value of these ideals on the basis of his own experience and practice, it is a waste. This truth has been forgotten by these personages. Let them awake in time and save the traditions and values of the ageless Vedic culture.

✧ ✧ ✧ ✧ ✧

12. Values In Later Texts

Soon after the propagation of Vedantha through the Upanishads and other texts, the Rishis, steeped in *tapas* (austerities) and the spiritual experience they gained therefrom, composed the Smrithis, expatiating upon the codes of conduct for the people, during the various stages of life as well as when they occupied various statuses in society. The Smrithis, however, did not acquire the authority that the Vedantic texts had, for they dealt with rights and responsibilities, duties and obligations.

Such Smrithis can be found in sacred scriptures being adored by followers of other religions. They consider such social codes and individual guidelines given by their Prophets and Seers as valuable and binding. We too revere them and should continue to revere them as regulations set up for the good of society and the progress of man. For, we must admit that they were framed by *Mahapurushas*, outstanding sages and well-wishers of the people.

But in the process of time, the Smrithis suffered change, by omissions and additions and by differences in emphasis. The sages allotted for each era or *Yuga*, a particular Smrithi, as authoritative. For, too many Smrithis, with divergent counsel, caused confusion and doubt. They said, those in the Kritha Yuga have to consider one Smrithi as specially laid down for them, that those in the *Thretha Yuga* have to follow the dictates of another, that in the *Dwapara Yuga*, people have to observe the path prescribed in a third and that the *Kali Age* people have to resort to a fourth. When centuries roll over the land one after another, new problems arise, new situations and predicaments confront man; and so the laws and limits of the past have to be altered here and there. Indeed, such adjustments are a part of the Design. The people have to be shown the path to spiritual progress, under the altered circumstances, and so the Smrithi that suits the new era is declared as binding.

Nevertheless *this* has to be borne in mind and carefully noted in memory by the readers. The Atma Dharma enunciated in the Vedantha, is eternal, unchangeable. It can never be watered down or "adjusted to the needs of the times." Faith in the Atma as the Core, the Reality, the Goal is the lasting teaching. It is true for all time. The truths of Atma Dharma are based on the eternal foundation of the core of *Purusha* and Prakriti, of Man and Nature which is the projection of the Divine Will. So, they are beyond the reach of change. They are as relevant and as valid today as they were thousands of years ago. Even when a thousand more years roll by, their relevance and validity cannot be affected in the least. Vedantha will stand firm irrespective of the past becoming the present and the present flowing on into the future.

The moral codes and ideals of good conduct, the sadhanas that man can adopt to control his mind and senses and purify his intelligence have, however, to suit the conditions of the people, the bonds they cultivate among themselves and other groups. With the changing face of social conditions, they too have to undergo adjustments and modifications. They could well be appropriate and beneficial under certain circumstances of time and space, but might be not so, under other circumstances. For example, the food regulations that are prescribed during certain periods are withdrawn and new rules laid down during certain other periods. Climatic conditions dictate the type of food needed. Smrithis recognise the need and allow changes in food habits, in order to maintain health. The same attitude is seen in other matters also. For the same reasons under modern conditions, it is desirable to have changes in the regulations and limits that govern society. Of course, the fundamental principles of Dharma must remain unaffected. They can never be shaken or loosened.

Now, about the Puranas. "*Puranam pranjali kshanam.*" That is to say, the Puranas deal with historical incidents of Creation and Evolution. The incidents are so chosen and narrated that they provide illustrations of basic philosophic truths. The Puranas were composed to expound the teachings of the Veda and Vedantha to the common man through interesting mythological and legendary tales. The language of the Vedas is very ancient and it contains many archaic elements of grammar and vocabulary. Even great scholars find it difficult to discover the age when the Rks were formulated. But the Puranas were composed in the language that was current and that was easily understood at the time. What we now know as the Sanskrit language is the language of the Puranas. Not only scholars but even ordinary folk could easily follow that language when the Puranas were written.

The Puranas have historical narratives of Divine Personages, great Rulers and Dynasties; and the fortunes of kingdoms and communities. Through them all can be seen shining examples of Dharma and expositions of spiritual principles.

All the texts, scriptures and holy books referred to are grouped under the one comprehensive name, "Hindu Sastras." It is no wonder that the people who revered and composed during thousands of years such a vast and valuable literature of religion and philosophy were, in course of time, divided and subdivided into sects and subsects, owing preferential loyalty to special creeds and beliefs. Some of these had broad gaps between them. We have no time now to elaborate on the fact that the differences between the sects are based on attitudes born out of the freedom of thought that was authoritatively allowed by the ancients. Nor is it necessary. What we have to grasp are: the truth accepted by all, and the attitudes approved by all, that is to say, the principles which a person calling himself "Hindu" has to believe.

What is exactly the Cause of Creation? What is the nature of the original Substance which Creation affected and how? These are questions important not only for Bharathiyas but for all men prone to inquiry. There can be no effect without a cause. There can be no structure without a base. Well, it can be asserted that all this visible Cosmos has Brahmam as the root cause. But what is Brahmam? Brahmam is eternal, pure, ever-vigilant, omniscient, indivisible, formless. Brahmam is the origin of this Cosmos or *Jagath*. Brahmam is shaping, evolving and fostering this Jagath.

Now, a few doubts might arise in people's minds: How is it that there is so much partiality evident in Creation? Some are born healthy and some others, unhealthy. Some lead prosperous, carefree lives, while others toil throughout their lives in dire poverty. Certainly, it can be argued, there are signs enough of the partiality that the Creation or Creator reveals.

It has to be made clear that life thrives on death. Life is based on death. One living thing consumes another, in order that it may live. The strong trample on the weak. This tale of terror continues unceasingly. That is the very nature of this world. Seeing this, people conclude that, if the world was created by God, He should be Cruelty itself. Such inference appears justified from the ordinary man's point of view. But the Bharathiya Paramartha Vahini, the Pure Stream of Bharathiya Spiritual Culture declares that this is not true at all! God is not the cause of either misery or joy, of good fortune or bad, it announces. Then, who brings about the evil and the good? The answer is—we ourselves. Rain falls equally on ploughed land and on unploughed. Only the ploughed land derives benefit therefrom. The clouds are not to blame. The fault lies in the ignorant idler who lets his land lie fallow. The Grace of God is ever at hand. It has no "more or less," no ups or downs. We draw upon it, more or less, or let it go by, or use it for our good.

The question might arise, "For what reason are some born in happiness and some in misery? They have done neither good nor evil, to be treated so unequally." True they have done nothing in this life, they are only just born. But they had done good or evil, in previous lives. The consequence of what was done in the previous life has to be experienced in this life.

Now, we can arrive at two conclusions on which all sects of Hinduism are agreed. The Buddhists and the Jains also accept these two. Every one of us has a firm belief, that life is eternal. It could not have originated from nothing. That is impossible. If it has come out of inert slime or mud, it would have been inert and inactive. All things put together will disintegrate. All that is bound by Time will end in time. If life started only yesterday, it cannot last beyond tomorrow. If it has roots, the roots shall go dry and the tree cannot survive forever. Life must have been existent ever since the Cosmos has been in existence. It does not require argument to understand truth. Do we not see that all modern sciences are tending to confirm more and more assuringly and clearly the revelations made in the texts and scriptures of Bharath? This too has to be accepted some day.

As authoritative texts of the basic beliefs of Bharathiya Culture in the spiritual field, the Upanishads, the *Brahma Sutra* and the *Bhagavad Gita*, the *Prasthana Thryas*, or the Three Sources, have to be reckoned. Many in India feel that the Adwaitha Vedantha alone is the correct one. But this attitude is not a correct one. The Upanishads are the very Voice of Easwara. The *Brahma Sutra* is the supreme embodiment of the principles and doctrine propounded by Vyasa. It is the most important of the texts depicting philosophic doctrines. It harmonises the entire body of philosophic beliefs. Though based on earlier texts and dissertations, there is no conflict between the earlier and later. In the aphorisms of the Brahma Sutras, each conclusion attains fulfilment and reconciliation. The *Bhagavad Gita* acts like a Commentary provided by God, for Vedantha.

All sects of Hinduism, who claim to be authentic and orthodox, accept the Three Sources as their basic texts—whether they are Dwaithins, Visishtadwaithins or Adwaithins (dualists, qualified-non-dualists or non-dualists). Whoever desired to propagate a new interpretation or a new attitude or theory—Shankara, Ramanuja , Madhwacharya , Vallabhacharya or Chaitanya—had to propagate it through commentaries from that standpoint on the Three Sources, the Prasthana Thraya only. Therefore, to assert that Vedantha can be used only with reference to the Upanishads and the doctrines that they teach will be a great mistake.

All conclusions drawn from the Prasthana Thraya are genuine and deserve the name Vedantha. Visishtadwaitha as well as Dwaitha have as much claim to be known as Vedantha as Adwaitha. This unity in diversity, this harmony in difference, this is the core of the current of Bharathiya thought.

There is milk in the body of the cow. The milk has ghee in it. But the cow cannot derive any strength through that ghee. The milk has to be taken out of the animal, it has to be boiled, and a little sour curd poured into it in order to curdle it. Then, when the milk is transformed into curds, it has to be churned and butter separated and rolled. Afterwards, the butter has to be melted and clarified, to get the ghee. The ghee thus prepared can be fed to the cow and then, it would be rendered stronger. So too, just consider—God is omnipresent. Yet, He is not amenable to man, unless man does sadhana.

There is oil in the sesame seed. There is butter in milk. There is water underground. There is fire latent in wood.

Similarly, the Omnipresent God is in the human body and the human mind. When we seek to separate him and identify Him, one has to make efforts and do sadhana. Then, as a consequence of the effort and the sadhana one will realise that God is oneself and there is no difference between the two. This is liberation, wisdom, realisation, according to Adwaitha. Sankara names this process the *Upasana* of Adwaitha.

Now, about the Upasana in Visishtadwaitha. Is the Sadhaka to consider the God whom he yearns to adore, as different and separate from him or as a part of him, associated somehow with him? This is the question. Now for the answer. The Jiva is the soul of the body. God is the soul of the Jiva. Having one's faith fixed thus, adoring God is the means that Ramanuja has propagated. All this Cosmos is part of Him. It is in Him. He is the inner Motivator and He is present in all. That Supreme Person can be known only through unflinching devotion, *Prapatthi, Saranagathi,* Total Surrender. "*Thwameva sarvam mama deva deva.* You are my all, Oh my God of Gods. You are my only Master,"—this is the attitude one has to develop and make one's own.

The Upasana (sitting near, steady worship) of Dwaitha—the Jivatma and the Paramatma relationship is as the wife-husband relationship. The Full Free Supreme Vishnu is the husband, the master, the lord, the ruler, the provider. The individual is the ruled, the dependent, the wife. This method of sadhana has been taught by Madhwacharya.

Without devoted attachment to the Lotus Feet of the Lord, that is to say, without Bhakthi, liberation from the cycle of Samsara, why even purity of intellect and emotions is impossible of attainment. For those who have the spring of ecstatic devotion to the Presence of the Lord within them, though they may not have any texts to ponder over, the very contemplation of the beauty, grace, and power of the Lord will give them bliss of superconscious Bhakthi. One cannot discover what prompts the experience. In that ecstatic mood, they discard all sense of shame and personality, and yearn to become the beloved of God, in blissful Union. They will then dance and sing aloud and be merged in genuine joy and ananda. Sadhana in conformity with this faith have been laid down by Madhwacharya. The agony of the lover to attain the beloved is the true sign of *Dwaithopasana* (Worship using external means, Dualistic philosophy). This has been elaborated in a thousand ways by others who came after.

The Upasana laid down in the Gita, is incorporated in the *Mahabharatha*, named as the Fifth Veda. The *Mahabharatha* is a veritable treasure house of gems illumining the problems that confront man in worldly and spiritual matters. The *Mahabharatha* is a magnificent drama that was enacted by Sri Krishna on the stage called Dharmakshetra (Field of Dharma), where He had collected together all the items he needed for the production. *Madhava*, that is to say, Krishna, was Director who collected the participants, the cast, the songs each had to sing, the words each had to utter and decided on the exits and entrances. He was the actor, the witness, the producer, all roles were He. On one side, immeasurable worldly power, soaked in unrighteousness, on the other side righteousness-filled, limited Atmic power. This is the essential charm of the *Mahabharatha*. This is the *Bhagavad Gita*. The entire essence of the *Mahabharatha* is in it. "*Karishye vachanam thava*"—"I shall do exactly as you order." "One can find safety and happiness in doing one's own duties"—"*Swadharme nidhanam sreyah.*" These are the touchstones of worldly Dharma.

Neglecting the path of Bhakthi which can add unto you all prosperity and progress, those who close their eyes and contemplate on "*Aham Brahmasmi*" "I am Brahmam," and suffer from the egoism it confers get only misery as their reward. If husk is pounded, no rice can be secured? Having no faith in Krishna's words, if one goes as his intellect dictates, it cannot be the road that leads to ultimate Truth, the *Brahma Thathwa.* The *Bhagavad Gita* has itself taught beyond the possibility of doubt, by means of illustrative descriptions and incidents that Krishna is Parabrahmam itself. It is the essence of all Vedanthas. It is the repository of the Amrith, the Nectar; churned out of the entire collection of Sastras. It is the sacred stream of Indian Spiritual Thought, held in one text. Is there anyone who can deny this?

✧ ✧ ✧ ✧ ✧

13. The Avatar As Guru

The cosmos or creation, time, karma or activity—all these are manifestations of the will of God and are bound to Him. They are considered by some as "false" and "unreal"; but how can God who is the very embodiment of Sathya or Truth "will" anything not true? Therefore, it can be said that these two are true, in one way. When evolution changes over into involution and the ultimate stage of mergence of both the conscious and the unconscious is reached, Easwara is the only One existent.

Time is the manifestation of the power of God, and so it has no end or beginning which can be measured. Karma too is an important Truth to be reckoned as such. Easwara is no wayward force, which is unmindful of bounds and limits. He creates situations and environments strictly according to the activities that men had engaged in during their previous lives. The Creation, the Time and the Karma—

all three are true in Easwara and true along with Easwara. They are instruments which He uses. They are bound to Him.

Easwara or God though not perceptible to the senses ordinarily, becomes so perceptible to the devotee who has such deep attachment to Him that he yearns to merge in Him. Why? Such devotees perceive God as clearly as they perceive external objects. God or Easwara is said to be Formless; that is to say, He can assume or adopt any form. He has endless Forms. Then, in what Form does He grant the clear Vision to the devotee? He manifests in the Form that the devotee yearns for, the Form which will grant him the highest satisfaction. These Forms are His Avatars. Easwara does not limit Himself when He thus manifests. He is fully present in every such Avatar. He manifests Himself with His full Glory in every Avatar.

It is said that there are some manifestations that are partial and some others that are full, and some that are temporary and some that are lasting. But these are called Avatars only by courtesy. Narada, Sanatkumara and other similar sages are referred to in some texts as such Avatars. They have not got all the Divine characteristics. Therefore, they are not worshipped.

The Jiva is by its very nature "eternal and immortal." It has no end or beginning that can be calculated. It has neither birth nor death. It is self-illuminating. It is the knower and the knowledge, the doer and the enjoyer. Whether bound or liberated, the Jivi has all these characteristics intact. But whatever it is, it has not got the Freedom that God has. In every act, the Jivi has to involve the body, the senses like the ear, etc., the vital airs that operate in the body. All these coexist with the Divine in the individual. Whatever it is, the Jivi is not a machine that has no will of its own. Just as the activities in this life are determined by the nature of the activities in previous lives, the activities of this life do determine the activities of the next life. Easwara decides the place and time, the circumstance and the consequence in accordance with the nature of the activities presently undertaken. God has the power to shape the Nature of man, but He does not exercise that power and mould it differently. He leaves it to the free will of the individual, which has to learn the lesson by experience.

The flake of stone that is chipped off the rock is a part of the rock; but the individual is not a part of God like that. In one sense, Jivi and Jagath are distinct and different from God. In another sense, they are inseparable. This mystery of separateness and identity cannot be grasped by means of reason and intellect. It can be understood only through the Vedas and their message. This is the main lesson that the *Sathya Sai Vahini* can instil.

Every child arrives into the world, bearing the burden of unrequited consequences, accumulated in previous lives. It does not drop from the lap of Nature, as a streak of lightning from the clouds. It is born in this world in order to experience the beneficial and the malignant consequences, that are the products of its own acts in past lives. This is the explanation for the differences that are evident among men. This is the principle of Karma.

Among men, each one is himself the cause of his fortune, good or bad. He is himself the builder, the architect. Fate, destiny, predetermination, the Will of God—every one of these explanations is toppled by the principle of Karma. God and man can be reconciled and affiliated only on the basis of this Sutra or principle of Karma. When man realises that God has no share in causing his suffering and that he is himself the sole cause, that no blame attaches to any other person, that he is the initiator as well as the beneficiary—the cause and the effect—of his acts, that he is free to shape his future, then he approaches God with a firmer step and a clearer mind.

If at the present time, a man is afflicted by misfortune, it is assuredly the result of acts done by him. Accordingly, man has to believe that happiness and good fortune also lie in his own hands. If he decides, happiness and good fortune can be gained by him.

If a person is pure in spirit now, he himself is the cause. Unless a person yearns, he cannot earn. So, it is clear that the will inherent in man is beyond all stages and conditions, all formations and transformations. The freedom that it represents, is the result of his past acts. It is powerful, infinitely fruitful and supreme.

The next problem is *Mukthi* or liberation. The Atma is neither masculine nor feminine. It is not possible to impose these distinctions on It. They are merely physical attributes, pertaining to the body. When talking about the Atma, ideas, such as these, are but signs of delusion. They are relevant only when the physical body is under discussion. The discussion of "age" is also a product of this delusion. The Atma is eternal. This ageless Entity is ever One and Only.

How did the Atma get incarnated? In the Sastras, there is just one explanation. For all this encasement and bondage, there is only one reason—*Avidya*, absence of right awareness. Through Avidya, man gets bound; so, wisdom is the cure. That alone can take him across. How can this awareness be accomplished?

There are three ways of acquiring it. Through Prema, through Bhakthi, through worship of God in full devotion and dedication, through loving service and adoration directed towards every living being who is but a moving temple of God—for He resides in each of them—the false knowledge, the Avidya can be scattered and the bonds made to fall off. The individual will then be released.

There are two ideas about God described in the Sastras—the idea that He is cognisable as having attributes and the idea that He is free from all attributes and so cannot be described as thus and thus, that is to say, the *Saguna* (Worship of God with attributes) aspect and the *Nirguna*

(Devoid of qualities, formless) aspect. The Saguna God is cognised as present everywhere, as the creator, sustainer and destroyer, of every thing and being, as the Father and Mother of the Universe. Therefore, He is beyond and above all beings and things and eternally distinct and different from man. It is said by upholders of the Saguna aspect that the very cognition of this attributeful principle brings about "liberation" or Mukthi. Liberation is attained when man establishes himself in this knowledge and lives in and through it.

The second way is the contemplation on the attributeless Nirguna principle. The truth that the ascription of attributes to the Divine principle is undesirable and inappropriate is realised during this contemplation and the attributes are shed from the concept of God. Then, the one Universal Attributeless person will alone remain in the consciousness. It can be referred to as the Knower, the *Jnatha*. For, Jnana or wisdom is relevant only in the context of the human mind and human consciousness. It cannot be designated as the Inquirer, for, inquiry is the mark of the weak. It cannot be related to the intelligence, for intelligence discriminates and the attempt to divide and dissect is again the sign of unsteadiness. It cannot be designated "the Creator," for creation is the activity of the bound, the limited. It or He has no bonds or limits. Activity implies a wish, a want, a desire; it does not originate from any other cause. All work has as its base some inner pain which is sought to be alleviated.

In the Vedas, the Divine is spoken of only as THAT. The reference is always to THAT. The word "He" is susceptible of provoking ideas of difference, and so the word THAT is used, to indicate that it is free from all limitations and bonds imposed by the ascription of attributes. This is the essence of the philosophy of non-dualism, for, attributes divide and distinguish.

It is the inescapable destiny of everyone to fulfil himself. Every living being has to attain fullness in the end. Each one is at present at a particular stage of this march, as a result of the activities engaged in during previous lives and the feelings he entertained in the past. The future is being built at present by the activities being engaged in now and the feelings that urge and shape them. That is to say, what we do, feel or think about, at present—these are the basic reasons for the good fortune or bad fortune which is in store.

The prompting to save oneself and the power to pull oneself up into liberation cannot be derived from books. This strength has to come from the individual himself. One can spend an entire lifetime scanning profoundly written books; one might earn the highest rank among intellectuals. But at the end of it all, one might not have attained even some little progress in the spiritual field. To conclude that a scholar who has reached the topmost height can therefore be considered ripe in spiritual wisdom will prove to be a great mistake. The scholar himself might imagine, as he learns more and more from books, that he is progressing more and more on the spiritual path. But when he examines the fruit of his studies, he will recognise that though his intellect has become sharper and heavier, he has not been acquiring the awareness of the Atma to the slightest degree. Most people have the skill to deliver wonderful discourses on spiritual subjects; really speaking, everyone has failed in living the life of the spirit, the *Paramarthika* (aspiration for the eternal) life. What exactly is the reason for this sad state of affairs? Now, spiritual texts are studied to equip oneself with scholarship in the competitive race for superiority, to earn one's livelihood, to pose oneself as an undefeatable upholder of some specific point of view, and generally, to earn a reputation as a pundit. The scholar might write elaborate commentaries on the Gita. But as a result of all that study, if in his character, behaviour and conduct, he does not prove that the Gita has soaked into him, all that punditry is but a burden he is carrying around. This is the lesson that Bharathiya culture tries to impress. The source from which this lesson emerges is the Guru, the Purusha, latent in you. The study of the scriptures and other texts can reinforce the spiritual urges already in man and induce him to practise the precepts. Do not treat the learning you derive from them as so much fodder for the brain. It must be sublimated into Ananda, for the individual. Envy, pompousness, egoism—such evil traits have to be driven out of the individual.

This spiritual treasure can be got from another too. Only, the giver has to possess supreme attainment, and the recipient has to possess the special merit that deserves the achievement. The seed may have life in it; but the soil must be ploughed and made fit to activate it. When both these conditions are satisfied, the harvest of spiritual success is assured. He who instructs in the field of religion has to be of enthralling excellence. The listener, too, has to be of sharp and clear understanding. When both are surprisingly supreme and extraordinarily enthusiastic, the result will be spiritual awakening of the highest level. Or else, rarely can such results follow. These are the real Gurus. They steal your hearts, not your wealth. The people have to concentrate on service to the Guru, and ruminate over his teachings. The pupil must be eager to translate the teaching into daily activity and actual practices. He must fill his heart with devotion and dedicate all his skill for the actualisation of the Guru's counsel. Such a person deserves the name, *Sishya* (disciple).

When the thirst for liberation and the revelation of one's reality is acute, a strange and mysterious force in Nature will begin operating. When the soil is ready, the seed appears from somewhere! The spiritual Guru will be alerted and the thirst will get quenched. The receiving individual has developed the power to attract the giver of illumination. That power is strong and full. Therefore, naturally the splendour that can confer the illumination will get ready to bless.

Readers! Though Gurus of the common type have increased in numbers, there is available for man, a Guru, far more supreme and far more compassionate than any or all of them. He is no other than the Avatar of the Lord. He can, by the mere expression of His Will confer on man the highest consummation of spiritual life. He can gift it and get man to accept it. Even the meanest of the mean can acquire the highest wisdom, in a trice. He is the Guru of all Gurus. He is the fullest embodiment of God as man. Man can cognise God only in the human form. The Bharathiya Spiritual Stream has been declaring, over and over again, that adoring God in the human form is the highest duty of man. Unless God incarnates as man, man can never hope to see God or listen to His Voice. Of course, man can picture God in various other forms, but he can never approximate to the genuine form of God. However much one may try, man cannot picture God in any form except the human. People can pour out wonderful discourses and talks on God and the nature and composition of all that exists in the Universe. They may satisfy themselves, asserting that all accounts of God descending in human form are meaningless myths. That is what the poor ordinary eye can discern. This strange inference is not based on Jnana. As a matter of fact, Jnana is absent in these assertions and declarations. What we can notice in them is only the froth floating on ego waves.

"*Koham*? Who am I?" "Why this feeling in me, that I am the doer?" "What is the nature of consciousness that I am the enjoyer?" "Why be born, and die at last?" "How did I deserve this life?" "Can I be liberated from this Samsara, this series of entrances and exits." The attempt to discover answers to these questions is what the Rishis of old designated as "thapas." When the intellect of the individual ripens into this steady inquiry, he enters the path of "thapas."

This is the first step. As soon as man has ascended this step, the Sastras or the collective wisdom of seekers enshrined in sacred texts, welcome him. The Sruthi, or the Vedas, directs him to "listen, ruminate, and practise" the axiomatic counsel of the sages. They assure him that he will attain the goal of release, and free himself from the delusive fascination for the visible world, portrayed for him by his own mind.

The Divine alone can be the guide, the companion and counsellor on this lone journey of man. Those styled Gurus cannot help or rescue. The Sruthis advise man to approach Gurus who are "*Srotriyas*" and "*Brahmanishtas.*" They warn man against resorting to others. What does Srotriya mean? It means a person who is unquestioningly loyal to the Sruthis or Vedas and who adheres to the rules prescribed and the limits imposed therein, without the slightest deviation. Brahmanishta means a person who is established by Brahma-consciousness. He has no doubts to pester him, no diversion to distract him. For, he has won steady faith in the Atma. He is unconcerned with the material world. He sees all worlds as Brahma, as the manifestation of the Brahma Principle. His activities and movements are in consonance with this awareness. His vision encompasses all of Time. He knows the past, present and the future. He is beyond all characterisation; the three (modes) do not affect him. He has his being in the One and Only—the Atma. He is unaffected by distinctions and differences, dualities and disparities. He is perpetually in Ananda.

The Vedas exhort the seeker to approach such a Guru. But only one Person has all these attributes. He is Sarveswara, the Lord of All. Scholars who have learnt the truth or are proficient in principles are not in the category of Srotriya and Brahmanishta. They are not the Gurus you need.

The Yogavasistha says that Sri Ramachandra asked the sage Vasishta the question, "Divine Master! Is there a way by which death can be avoided?" This same problem drove Gautama Buddha along the path of renunciation, and forced him to give up all traces of attachment. It showered on him eternal fame, as supreme among men. Prahlada, foremost among the devotees of the Lord, addressed his fellow pupils, even as a boy, "Friends! Have you not observed some boys of our own age fall dead and get burnt or buried?" Thus, he drew their attention to the event of death and invited them to draw lessons from that inevitable fact. He taught them the higher wisdom.

Those who have the inner urge to achieve the higher wisdom which confers liberation have, therefore, to reflect upon and investigate the phenomenon of death. Death should arouse no fear. It should not be regarded as inauspicious. You should not run away from the problem, imagining that death happens only to others, and that it will not happen to you. Neither should you postpone reflections on death, judging that they are inappropriate now, and profitless. For, inquiry into death is really inquiry into one's own Reality. This truth has to be recognised.

Viveka (discrimination), the special gift to man, has to be employed to unravel the reality of the visible Universe, its nature and validity. The fact of death is the prime cause which originates the problem. "Who am I?" So, that fact ought not to be ignored, as unworthy of attention. You should not flee from it in fear. For, if you behave so, you land yourself on the first step towards *Ajnana*, stupidity, and plant in your mind the seedling of the tree of foolishness. You prop up the pillars of Maya.

Every mystery latent in human existence is entwined with the inquiry into death. The glory and majesty of the Divine are fully revealed only when death is investigated. Among the three boons that Nachiketa asked for from Yama, the God of Death, the chief was, according to the *Kathopanishad*, the one relating to death. "Does man exist after death? Some persons declare that he does, some others assert that he does not. Each argues as his fancy leads. Which of these opinions is true? Solve this problem for me," pleaded Nachiketa, and insisted on an answer. Yama tried to avoid his pleading. He said, "Son! Nachiketa! This is an insoluble mystery. The sacred texts treat it as subtler than the subtlest. I find it impossible to make even the gods understand this phenomenon. Nevertheless, you are craving for this boon! Why should you be troubled by this problem? You are an innocent little boy. You deserve to live long, enjoying many a happy event. I shall grant you, as boon, enormous riches; accept them and lead a life of unexcelled happiness. Ask for any quantity of material pleasure, they are yours. Come, ask and reach the height of joy."

But Nachiketa replied, "Dharmaraja! However vast the riches, however pleasant the experiences they confer, they have to receive your impact without a murmur? Nothing in creation can escape you, can they? Everything is immersed in death. Why then should I aspire for items that give only temporary relief? Grant me the boon on which my heart is set." In the *Mahabharatha*, Dharmaraja is asked to answer the question, "Name the greatest marvel in the world." And, Dharmaraja replied, "Though we see every day people dying, we do not think we would ourselves die. What can be a greater marvel than this?" Similarly, Yajnavalkya, the famous sage, after deciding that he would join the monastic order, called before him, his two wives—Katyayani and Maitreyi, and informed them that he had partitioned his movable and immovable properties, equally, for both of them. On hearing this, the elder wife, Maitreyi, who was endowed with a high level of intelligence and insight, protested and said, with a smile on her face, "Lord! Can these riches you are handing over to me save me from death and render me immortal? If you assure me that they will do so, certainly I shall accept them, with due reverence to you." Yajnavalkya explained,

"Riches make life pleasant and delightful by the chances they give you to live happily. Do you say that you do not need such valuable riches?" But Maitreyi persisted. She said, "If what you say is true, you could have continued enjoying these riches and deriving happiness therefrom. Why have you decided to give them up and become a monk? No, it is not proper to cheat us, weak-minded women, holding forth before us these delusive trinkets. How can the riches, which *you* refuse to keep, give *us* peace and happiness? These are temporary objects. They are liable to destruction. They entangle us still further in bondage. They foster the ignorance which we yearn to discard. They are the chief promoters of anxiety and worry. They are basically polluted, since they are not within the realm of the Atma." When Maitreyi placed before him this truth, Yajnavalkya was silenced. Not knowing how to proceed, he stood with his head bent before her. Then, Maitreyi fell at the feet of her husband, and said, "Lord! You are master of all mysteries. You must have called us and placed before us this proposal, in order to test our intelligence. I have no desire for luxury or even comfort. I do not crave for riches and possessions. Instruct me, about the path that can confer eternal Bliss." In fact, there is only ONE—the Parabrahma. The Adwaitha Sastras proclaim "*Brahma sathyam; jagat Mithya; Jeevo Brahmaiva naaparam.*" "Brahmam alone is true. Creation is a myth. The Jivi or the individual is Brahmam Itself." All that happens in the world to man is as unreal as the dream-experience. They disappear, and appear again. The pleasures and joys experienced in life are as mirages appearing on the desert sands of hatred, envy and selfish greed. Now, how can those persons who believe that this mirage is real and run towards it, become Gurus? Will it be proper to address them as Jnanis, the Wise? They are installed on high seats of illusory authority. They teach what they do not practise. They hold forth ideals which they themselves ignore. How can such persons be examples to seekers who need spiritual progress? They are not genuine, for, they have not even an iota of the Guru principle in them.

Sarveswara, or the Lord, alone, is the genuine Guru. For all seekers, this is the path. Let them hold fast to this faith.

✧ ✧ ✧ ✧ ✧

14. This and That

Every living being refers to itself as "I," "I." "I am Ramayya," "I am Krishnayya," "I am Sita," "I am Radha." Each one, assumes the "I," as his own, and uses it whenever he has to designate himself. If only birds, beasts and other living things could speak, they too would have behaved likewise and referred to themselves as "I." Besides these, even mountain peaks, hills and trees might announce themselves as "I am hill," "I am anthill," "I am tree," if only they could speak.

When we spend some time thinking over this, it will be clear that some great mystery is embedded in this expression, I. The illiterate boor uses this expression. The sage who has secured the Divine vision uses It. Even God, it is said, announces Himself as I. Nevertheless, who probes into this mystery? And among those who have dared probe, how many have succeeded in unravelling it? And even if there are a few who have unravelled the mystery, how many among them have used the discovery to transform their lives? Have the celebrated intellectuals, the Pundits, the Paramahamsas succeeded in delving into the meaning and significance of this "I"?

No, let us see whether the exponents and commentators of the *Bhagavad Gita*, who can reel off the eighteen chapters and the seven hundred slokas in a continuous stream, have grasped the full implications and importance of the word, "I." In the Gita, the declarations by Sri Krishna—"*Aham moksha-yishyami*—I shall absolve you," "*Maam ekam saranam vrja*—Come to me, the One, for refuge" "*Kshetrajnam cha api maam viddhi*—And, also know Me, as the knower of the Field," and the like—He refers to "I," does He not? So, this expression "I" is clearly omnipresent. It is the sign and symbol of all Jivatmas. It has unlimited forms and appearances. Like the string that passes through the rosary beads, it interpenetrates and holds together all names and forms.

However transient names and forms might be, the "I" persists without being affected. Therefore, one has to know this omnipresent "I" so that one can understand all that has to be known. He who has known it is the *Jagad-guru*, (the World-teacher), the *Viswa-guru*, (the Teacher of all Beings), the *Sadguru* (the Teacher to be followed).

The body is but the container, the *Upadhi*, the sheath. Nevertheless, imposing differences and distinctions based on physical characteristics and material considerations, some are elevated as "touchable" and some condemned as "untouchable"; some are classified as "high" and others as "low." Intellect cannot claim honour, and persons cannot claim to be Pundits if studies are directed to the amassing of money or earning the wherewithal for a comfortable living. Nor can skill and excellence in argumentative scholarship be worthy of reverential mention. Really, the word "I" leads you to the Supreme Godhead, when you dive into its significance. "That is you," "That is I," "I and That are One," this is what the great Vedic dictum, "*Thath thwam asi*—That thou art"—declares. That is the very core of all teaching, the grandest of counsels.

This sacred principle embodied in the "I" is beyond the grasp of the most learned scholars, by means of lone inquiry, without guides and helpers. Only, the guides have to be those who are aware of the Truth and who are earnest in living the Truth. It is beyond the reach of scholarship, logic and grammar. Note that these are warnings administered by the Sruthis and the Smrithis.

Well, when one intends to learn in a general way about this "I" and its implications, he can be told the secret in just three sentences: "I am active in day time, when I am awake. I sleep at night. I experience dreams when I sleep. Thus, acting and experiencing both day and night, I die." When one considers these statements of the individual, one can conclude that they are based on the individual's knowledge gained from this life. "The 'I' begins when I am born," he believes. But did this "I" exist before birth? If it had, how can an existing thing be said to be born? Even if this objection is ignored, how did it exist and where? Was it disembodied apart from name and form? Was it beyond the pale of the senses? Doubts such as these pursue the seeker in waves. It has to be understood clearly that the "I" is not related or affixed to one object, thing, or being, to one name and form. Remember this when you identify and recognise the "I" or arrive at the true answer to the question, "Who am I?" you have identified and recognised the entire Cosmos and its mysteries.

It may be asked, what exactly is the urgency to understand the meaning of this "I" when there is an infinite number of topics that call for study in the Universe? One can well try to unravel the secrets of the Cosmos. Or, attention may be paid to understand what is meant by "Jivi," or, by "Deva" (God). When such profound subjects as the Universe, the Individualised Divine, the Divine itself—subjects that are incomparably important—are clamouring for attention, why give them up and investigate the meaning of expression used by common folk and children, this "I," "I"? Of what benefit can it be? People may ask.

The expression is simple, of course; but its implications are infinite, and fundamentally satisfying. This is the reason why all great teachers exhort the seekers, "Know thyself," "Inquire into yourself, that alone can give you release." The

Sastras too confirm this exhortation. "*Yad Vijnaanena Sarvam vijnaathaṃ bhavathi*—That, which when known, everything becomes known." The Sastras extol the importance and value of this inquiry, and make it clear that the inquiry into the Atma is essential. The assurance is given that the Atma is you, yourself, as in the sacred axiom, "Thath thwam asi. That thou art."

Therefore, to fulfil the yearning, you have first to inquire into this mystery, who you are. You can then realise that you are *nitya*, eternal, beyond the boundaries of Time. The Sastras will help you to cast away the Ajnana, the dark clouds of ignorance that now hide this Truth from your awareness. Then, you can delight at the experience of the awareness of your genuine Nature. The awareness comes when the Truth is revealed with the dawn of light. But the Sastras which guide man into the knowledge of these great mysteries and into the region where such bliss can be secured are not studied now. Instead, man pursues with blinkered eyes his own silly notions. How then can he attain the Atmic Principle? How then can he reach the very embodiment of Ananda?

Mere worldly scholarship cannot delve into the meaning of the Sruthis. The Grace of God has to be won by devotion and dedication, and that Grace alone, the compassionate Glance of the Eye of God alone, can instil into him the real meaning of the Sruthis. Only persons who are embodiments of Divine wisdom and Compassion can decide what exactly is helpful to the spiritual progress and well-being of man.

Others only flounder. They will find it impossible to cope with the task. For, how can Gurus who fail to save themselves, help in saving others? The Gurus of today endeavour to cleanse society while their own houses are unclean. The number of such Gurus is increasing; and so, faults and failures are multiplying. Their haltings justified and explained away, in various ways, and so the confusion grows worse. As a consequence, endless argumentation ensues and Reality is lost to view. These Gurus interpret the Sastras to suit their prejudices and partialities, making them instruments for their aggrandisement.

Under these distressing conditions, the Grace of God is the only hope of man; that is the beacon to illumine the path. That is the compassion which rewards man for his spiritual struggle. That is the strong steady ship that can take him safely across.

Many preceptors and teachers declare that the path of inquiry into oneself is the path of liberation for man, "*Swa vimarso mokshah*—Self-inquiry leads to Liberation" is the assurance. "That is the Atma; that is my Self," "I" and the Atma are not different." "The Atma and the Paramatma are not separate." The yarn "I" is both warp and woof of the cloth, the Atma. When the "I" yarn is found in different bodies and feels that in each body it is distinct from the rest, the Atma cloth can be said to disappear; but in both yarn and cloth, there is one substance ever persisting, in spite of how each feels—and that substance is "cotton."

So too, Paramatma persists as the only Truth, in the "I," the Atma. Without the cotton, Paramatma, there can be no "I" yarn. Without the "I" yarn, there can be no Atma cloth. These three—Paramatma, Atma and I—are only forms and names for the ONE—the Paramatma, the ONE Atma, the DIVINE Atma.

✧ ✧ ✧ ✧ ✧

15. Levels and Stages

"The Hindu religion authorises the worship of a variety of Gods. This has resulted in sectarian feuds and factions which fill the land with fear and unrest." All the infights and agitations in the country can be traced to this one basic defect—this is the unthinking verdict of many observers. But this judgement is not correct. It is a flimsy flight of fancy, indulged in by persons devoid of the faculty of reason.

In the West, the inhabitants of all lands are, more or less, adherents of the Christian religion. Though all of them adore one God, they have been slaughtering each other by methods far more horrible than wild animals resort to. Do they not wage wars in which people remote from the scene of conflict including innocent women, children and the aged are wiped off the earth by merciless fire-power? Is their religion the basic cause for such heartless, disgraceful, stupid and demoniac devastation and fratricide? Of course, they belong to one religion and they adore one God, but there must be some poisonous trait lurking behind the facade of adoration, polluting the entire personality. Religion cannot be the cause even to the slightest extent, for factions, fights, and wars.

Germany had no place for caste groups and sectarian conflicts. It had achieved extraordinary progress in science and technology. It shone in the forefront of nations by means of its strength, courage and heroism. Such a nation was cut up into four bits by the four victorious powers each bit being ruled by a separate nation! Japan which has no problems of religious differences and sectarian conflicts had to suffer the vengeance of the nations for some years! What was the reason? For the downfall of nations, religion alone cannot be the cause.

No one can even imagine a world in which differences do not exist. Differences are born from the inner springs of intelligence and the cumulative effect of impacts. The life of every being is the external expression of this intelligence and this effect. Inert as well as non-inert entities are but manifestations, on different levels, of this intelligence. The parrot casts its eyes in a distinct way. The crow does the same, quite differently. The jackal reasons out situations differently from the dog. The nature of animals is of one type. The nature of human beings is of another type. Between man and man, there are differences in the knowledge gained.

Not only in knowledge but even in physical characteristics and personal charm, there are countless variations. Their likes and dislikes, their thoughts and feelings are shaped in diverse ways by the knowledge they have and the professions they are engaged in. We have no need to go so far. Even twins growing together in the same womb are not often identical. They manifest different natures. What is the reason for this? The reason lies in differences in the development of the intelligence.

Therefore, at no time can mankind be free from differences. Universal equality is an impossible aspiration. The desire to have it established on earth is a fantasy. It is a search for flowers in the sky.

The animal lives with the awareness that it is an animal, the bird has the consciousness that it is a bird. A woman engages herself in the activities of the world, conscious that she is a woman; so also does man. The consciousness one has, until sleep overwhelms, continues without change after waking from sleep. The living being continues his activities as before sleep. Man continues his activity where it was broken off by sleep. So too, man continues in this life, the activities broken off by death, from where they were ended. "*Yam, Yam vaapi smaran bhaavam, thyajathyanthe kalebaram*. He gives up his body at the end, remembering the feelings that moved him ever so strongly." And in the Gita, "*Tham thamaivethi Kauntheya, sadaa thad bhaava bhavithah*—He attains that status itself to which his feelings were all the while directed." The nature of the next life is in accordance with feelings which occupy the mind when man casts off his corpse. For, those feelings will only be in accordance with the feelings that motivated his living days. On deeper thought, it will be evident that the basic truth is just this: everything depends on the progress attained in the sublimation of intelligence.

Though in outer form, a certain uniformity may appear, there exist vast and varied differences in inner nature. A genus or species is mainly decided on outer characteristics, which are really the manifested expressions of the inner intelligence. An individual is primarily a form. Man, tree, hill, sparrow, fox, dog, cow, snake, scorpion—these "sounds" denote members of the species with these forms. The individuals may undergo destruction, but the species will continue. Men may die, but mankind will persist. Trees may fall and be reduced to ash or dust but the genus cannot ever suffer destruction. The living genus is eternal, total destruction can never happen.

If we analyse and inquire into even the small things that we experience in our daily lives, these truths will be clearly evident before us. We say that everyone in the human species has human characteristics but when we evaluate one person, we pay special attention to his virtues and habits, present status and future prospects.

Cows—all of them—belong to one species. But when we desire to purchase a cow, we try to find out its parentage.

We look for auspicious marks on the body. It must give us plenty of milk. It must be a pretty, little, quiet animal. We purchase only cows with these desirable qualities. We are not attracted by the fact that it is a cow like the rest of the species. We do not purchase a barren cow or a wild unruly cow. Therefore, though all men are more or less uniform, one is to be evaluated on the basis of one's qualities only.

When an inquiry in depth is made into another topic, it will be clear that feelings of difference between high and low are natural reactions. Though urine and faeces are uniformly unclean, the urine of the cow is treated as holy. Sanctity is not attributed to the urine or faeces of other animals; these are definitely unholy. Take the instance of fire, Agni. Fire is fire, whatever the form. We light lamps at home. We have fire in our hearths. We have the sacrificial fire, rising up in flames. This Agni is revered and worshipped; people prostrate before it. But the fire in the lamp and the hearth are not evaluated so high. When fire is raised to burn a corpse on the cremation ground, the flame is not considered pure enough for any other use. No one will bake "rotis" (Indian wheat bread) over it; no one will revere it or offer prostrations before it. For, it is treated as "low," "unholy," "polluted."

Similarly, though men have the same physical form, the peculiarities of each body and of the other sheaths in which he is encased, and the nature of his qualities and activities, distinctions among them have necessarily to be made. Some must be treated as "high" and some, as "low." Electric bulbs do not all emit the same quality of light. Some are bright and some dull. There is the same current in every bulb though some express it in full strength and others are not able to do so.

We have to accept that for the world to evolve, levels of awareness, stages of excellence, distinctions like high and low, holy and unholy, religious and irreligious are essential requisites. They are inevitable. They are designed by Divine Will.

✧ ✧ ✧ ✧ ✧

16. Man and God

For the consummation of human evolution, and the realisation by man of his highest goal, religion and spiritual discipline are very essential. Religion is the link between the individual and the Universe, between JIVA and DEVA. If that does not exist, life becomes chaos. A cow caught on a hill, wanting to go to the hill opposite, but confronted with a flooded river in between, needs a bridge between the two. That is what religion is. Between the hill of individual life and the region of the Universal, there is the flooded river of Nature, with all its confusion and complexities. It is difficult to discover where it comes from, how it accumulates all that uproar and where it ultimately ends. But fortunately, we have in every human community bridge-builders, who help people to cross.

We may have more than one bridge, but the purpose of each is the same. The bridge built by the sages and seers of India is known as the Sanathana Dharma bridge. It is called so because it is an eternal, everlasting bridge based on the ageless foundation of the Vedas, and can be reliably used by all, in all countries, at all times. That is why it is sometimes called the Vedic bridge and the Vedic path, also as the Aryan Path. All attempts to trace those who have laid this path have failed. This is the reason why they have given up the search in despair, characterising the path as "*akartha*" or undesigned. They assured themselves that the Vedas or in other words the Lord himself has been the designer.

All religions and spiritual paths laid through the ages are indeed sacred; for, they have all been designed by Messengers of the Lord, chosen because they are the foremost of men. Buddha, Jesus Christ, Zoroaster, Mohammed—names such as these are known world wide. Their doctrines, ideals, and thoughts, have all become so valid for their followers that their names have been identified with their religions.

Since the ideal religion at that time was believed to be the Message from God and since that Message was communicated and spread by Jesus Christ his name was given to it. So also the Buddhist religion was named after Buddha, since it was intuited and spread through him as the Divine instrument. Mohammed who heard the Message of God laid down doctrines and disciplines and those who follow them are said to belong to Mohammedanism. Therefore it is not wrong to say that all these religions are products of the foremost among men and the most ideal Messengers of the Lord.

Divine Intelligence is universal and all-comprehensive. Human intelligence is confined within narrow limits. Its range is very poor. The scriptures deal with only one goal, but they indicate different paths to reach it. Each path could be a definite religion and its doctrines and disciplines considered different from the rest. So the statement that Rama, Christ, Zoroaster, Buddha, Mohammed, and others are one, is not valid.

In the Christian religion, it is stated that individual beings were created as they are. It is said that Allah did the same. Even Zoroastrian and Buddhist religions describe creation more or less on the same lines. But Vedic religion has a different version. The individual is as eternal as God. He is a spark of God. If there are no jivis (beings) there is no Deva (God). This is specially emphasised in the Vedas. Followers of other religions are, in recent times, recognising this truth. The present life of each is only an interval between the previous and the future lives. It is but a step towards the next. This is indicated in the Vedas. The Vedas instruct about the relationship between the previous and future births. No other religion however, has revealed so much about previous and future births.

Another point: Among the four objectives of life, Dharma, Artha, Kama and Moksha, various religions describe the stage of Moksha or liberation in various ways.

Each one lays down some doctrine and insists upon faith in that doctrine. And therefore there is no agreement or identity between the experiences they describe. The Hindu description of the experience can however be gained by followers of all religions. There may be agreement in the details of the descriptions in various religions. But the total experience is not described in the same manner. The reason is: Hindu religion which has come down from the timeless past is really supreme. Other faiths are only based on some of the doctrines of Hinduism selected by them and developed in accordance with the traditions and culture of their own region. Therefore Truths inherent in the Hindu faith often appear in those other faiths. Hinduism and Hindu culture have been flowing as one continuous stream.

In the Hindu religion rituals and ceremonies have been laid down to be observed from sunrise to nightfall without any intermission. Many of them are elaborate *yajnas* (inward-directed sacrifice), *yagas* (outward-directed sacrifice), and sacrificial offering to Divine Powers. Not being content with rituals and dedicatory ceremonies appropriate to the baby growing in the womb until death and the subsequent attainment by the person of higher worlds, elaborate disciplines have been laid down. No other religion has so many and so elaborate rules of living. Therefore, it will not be correct to declare that all religions are the same. They might have adopted a few or many of these from Hinduism since Hinduism has, from the beginning, laid emphasis on them.

In order to carry out this heavy schedule of Karma or ritual, man must have Bhakthi, Jnana and Yoga—Faith, Understanding and SELF-CONTROL. Dharma is the tap root of the great tree, religion. It is the eternal source of its strength. It is fed by waters of Bhakthi. The leaves and flowers are renunciation and other virtues, and the fruit is Jnana.

In these stages of growth, if there is any interruption or deficiency, that is to say even if any regulation is missed the fruit of wisdom or Jnana which the tree yields will be affected adversely.

Such strict plans for spiritual progress can be found only in Hinduism and not in any other faith. For Hinduism is the nectar churned and prepared by the ancient Rishis out of their own genuine experience. It is not put together from things available in books.

It is not proper for anyone to adopt whichever faith or code that pleases him most. For they believe that life is a matter of just three days, and so they need morality and self-control. Life is a long journey through time, and religion confers peace for the present and encouragement for the future. We must believe that we are at present undergoing the consequences of our own activities in the past.

It is a great source of peace that people can be content with their present conditions because they know they themselves were the cause and know that if one does good and meritorious deeds now, it is possible to build a happy future. This is great encouragement. It is only when life is run on these two lines that morality and self-control can have a place in life. The power to adhere to these two ideals consists in the encouragement and the enthusiasm given by religion.

We cannot determine the origin of religion or its end. So also it is difficult to declare the origin and the end of the individual or the Jiva. According to Hinduism a Jivi is timeless, the present life is but the latest of the series brought about by its own thoughts and acts. The Jivi has not come now, as a result of either the anger or the grace of God. They are not the cause of this present existence. This is the declaration made by the Sanathana Dharma.

Religion cannot be, at any time, a mere personal affair. It may be possible to assert so, since each one's faith is rooted in himself and since each one expresses that faith in his own behaviour and actions. But how far is that statement valid? It is not valid to assert that there is no God or religion or *Varna* (caste), as many intelligent people do to their own satisfaction. We find a large number of people proclaiming the non-existence of God and declaring that the directives to guide and sublimate one's activities laid down in all religions are superstitions. These persons are not ignoramuses. They are not without education. When such individuals characterise spiritual beliefs and practices as superstition, what importance can we attach to their statements! If they entertain such convictions in hearts, society need not complain, for it suffers no harm. But they do not stay quiet. For example, intoxicating drinks like toddy, brandy, etc., are indulged in by others. Can this be dealt with as if it is a personal affair? Do others feel happy over it? However emphatically the matter is declared "personal," this evil habit does affect society subtly and openly in various ways. It demonstrates its nefarious effects, in spite of everything. When ordinary persons indulge in such harmful habits, the danger is not so considerable. But when elders who have won a name in society do so, the common man too follows the evil path.

The works of Vyasa and Valmiki are very ancient. Such writings of past ages are aptly called Puranas. But though centuries have flown by since they were born, age is powerless to affect them. Had it been otherwise, they would not be loved and demanded even today by people residing all over the land from the Himalayas to Sethu. The texts are so young and fresh. They are unaffected by the passage of time. Whoever desires Ananda at whatever place, whenever he needs, can get himself immersed in it.

The *Manu Dharma Sastra* is unique. We have no text to compare with it in any country throughout history. Can anyone create a book of the same type at any time? The doctrines of the Hindu faith and the Sastras which enshrine them do not offer homage to material sciences. These do, of course progress from day to day but the theories honoured one day are condemned the next day and new theories are brought up to explain the same phenomenon. How then can the eternal and ever-valid truths of the spirit honour the material sciences? The scientists of today call this attitude "blind faith." They want it to be discarded. They want every subjective and objective fact to be examined and put to rigorous tests. They confuse themselves when they consider this as an independent path to the discovery of reality. But it is not correct. There is no need to dig up and lay bare new doctrines. Every principle and path is readily available. Understanding is the only thing we need aspire to.

Western philosophers from Kant to Spencer have, in fact, only dwelt upon some facets of the Dwaitha, Adwaitha and Visishtadwaitha schools of thought. Hindus have long ago delved into these matters and reduced their understandings into doctrines and principles.

✧ ✧ ✧ ✧ ✧

17. Colour and Caste

Hindu Dharma and its rules of life are based on Varna (caste) and *Asrama* (stage of life). Let us take first the principle of Varna in religion. The word Maya used in Vedantha discussions has generally been the target for indifference, neglect and criticism. So too Varna. Varna and the distinctions based on it are condemned as the artifices of man. Maya is condemned likewise as against all reason, for it disregards the world calling it illusion. The Smrithi declares, "*Chaathur varnyam, maya srshtam*" (the four varnas are created by Me); the Sruthi says, "*Brahmanosya mukham aseeth; baahooraajanyah krthah,* etc." (The *Brahmin* emerged from the face, the *Kshatriyas* rose from the arms). It is clear Varna is created by the Lord. Nevertheless, if it is propagated that the Varna system has brought about disastrous distinctions, the fault lies in misinterpreting the word.

Are there in society now genuine Varnas? What exactly is Varna? Is any attempt made to discover that fact? No. Varna is just a word. Every word has a meaning and Varna too ought to mean something, should it not? To prove that trees exist, the word "tree" is enough. A word is just sound but it indicates something existing. The sound "elephant" is the proof of the existence of that animal. So too, when the sounds, "cat," "dog," "fox" are heard, the forms of those animals present themselves before the mind's eye. The sounds were there even before us. We were born into the tangle of sounds. We did not originate them. We require groups of men and things if there is a wish to originate sound and shape it into a meaningful word. So, for every current word, a meaning must adhere. We cannot impose on it the meaning we choose. The words with their implications are there already, even before our birth. We just use them, whichever way we want, whenever we need.

Word involves speech. It means *Pada*, in Sanskrit. Every object in the world is called in Sanskrit, a "*Padaartha*," "word-meaning." The hill is the heap of earth indicated by the word "hill." Similarly, the word Brahmin and *Sudra* inform us that there were persons answering to those words. The questions "Who is a Brahmin? Who is not a Brahmin?" are irrelevant now. What is being made known is only the conceptions of "word" and "meaning." The entire Cosmos is subsumed under "word" and "meaning"; it is sheer Name and Form (the Name being the Word, and the Form, the Meaning).

The Sruthis (Vedas) declare so. "*Vaachaa-rambhanam Vikaaro Naamadheyam.*" "Name and Form are one single indivisible unit" just as Shiva and Parvathi, Active and Inert, Object and Image, the Moon and Moonlight. Yet, for dealing with the world, the Word is all-important. The word arises from thought. Thought is shaped by experience. Experience depends on desire and desire springs from Ignorance, Ajnana, Maya, Avidya or Prakriti, which too is fundamentally based on the Divine.

Since it is based on the Divine Lord who is the Splendour of Wisdom, the repository of Innate Glory, the darkness of Maya, Ignorance, Avidya or Prakriti should not overpower us. Where light is present, darkness has no place. The Lord declared, "I shall become Many" and that Will resulted in the Cosmos and is directing It forever. Therefore, Name and Form are the results of that Will, and not of any human will. It will be an absurd claim if man pretends that He originated them. The All-powerful Lord alone has willed so. That is the reason why He is designated as the Supreme. To the question, "Does God exist?" the existence of the word God is the indisputable proof.

The world consists of multifarious objects and each has a name. No one has discovered how or why these names get attached to these objects. Nor is it possible to explain the how and why. Even if an attempt is made, the result can be only a guess and not the truth. So it is best to conclude that it is divinely descended. Words used between birth and death, or current before birth or after death, words indicating the mother and the children, or words like Righteousness (Dharma), Unrighteousness (Adharma), Heaven *(Swarga)* and Hell (Naraka) are certainly not human artifices but divine dispensations. The Vedas are the authority for this declaration.

Let us consider one point. Can anyone quote a single instance either in this world or some other of a mere word which does not convey a meaning? No. It is impossible. Each word has a meaning. That meaning denotes a decision by God. It is only when this is recognised by men that they can grasp the mystery of life.

So when it is declared that the Brahmin manifested from the face "*Brahmanaasya mukham aaseeth*" or that the four varnas have been created by Me, *chaathur varnaym Mayaa Srshtam*, does it not also posit that there must have been Varnas which are denoted by the word and persons who could be described as examples of representatives of that word? Do not these declarations make plain to us that the very God who created them grouped them on the basis of their tendencies and activities as Varnas?

So the word Varna can be understood in all its bearings only if deep inquiry is made and clean thought is directed on it. The meaning of Varna, the most common among the people and current everywhere, is "colour." But how this word came to be attached with that meaning is not known to many. This has to be known in order to grasp the true significance of the word. In the word Varna, the root *Vr* means "description" "elaboration," also the process of "counting." The roots r, rn, which form such words as *ramana* mean "enjoyment, pleasure, etc." Therefore, Varna signifies "accepting with pleasure after elaborate consideration."

As regards "colour" white, red and black are the basic ones. Other colours are but derivatives. The white symbolises the Sathwic tendency, the red, the Rajasic and the black, the Thamasic. That is the mystery of creation. Individuals take birth according to the tendencies they appreciate, aspire for and adopt. So the Varnas into which they are born are determined by themselves and not by any external authority. Which particular tendency they choose to cultivate depends on their intellectual level. It is generally believed that desires shape the intelligence. Intelligence moulds the activities and activities decide the character and nature of life. This is the correct interpretation of the expression "*Guna* (quality, attribute) *Karma Vibhaagasah*." While the Sruthi and the Smrithi texts indicate so elaborately the causes that lead to the individual's birth, life and death in particular castes, religion, families and sections, persons who are unable to understand the same lay down theories according to their own limited intelligence and derive satisfaction therefrom.

What else is this but sheer ignorance? Or it may be egoist pride exhibiting that they know everything, for, is not egoism itself the progeny of ignorance? The conclusion is that caste, social status, family and even religion are determined by *Guna* (quality, attributes) and Karma. They are not amenable to human manipulation. The Vedas declare so. They posit that it has been so decided by Divine Will.

Bharath is designated as *Karma-bhoomi*, or *Karma-Kshethra*, the Holy Land of Godward Activity. All men everywhere are pilgrims trekking towards the Holy Land of Godward Activity. Karma is the *sine qua non* of Bharath. It holds forth the divinity of activity and turns all activity into spiritual sadhana. This is the reason for the names by which Bharath is known.

The sacred scriptures of this land (Sruthi) loudly proclaim that the individual is the architect of his own fate, high or low status in society, luxury or poverty, liberty or bondage. "*Sa yatha Krathurasmin loke purusho bhavathi; thathe thah prathye bhavathi*": "Whatever form the person craves for now while alive in this world, that form he attains after death": Sruthi declares thus. Therefore it is clear that Karma decides Janma, and that the luxury or poverty, the character and attitude, the level of intelligence, the joys and grief of this life are the earnings gathered during previous lives. The inference therefore is inevitable that the next life of the individual will be in consonance with the activities prompted by the level of intelligence which rules the person here and now. Some persons though of noble birth engage themselves in evil deeds. Others, though born in castes considered low, are engaged in good deeds. How does this happen? This is a problem that agitates us often. Persons born as Brahmins perform bad deeds; in other words, they descend into Rajasic and Thamasic levels. Persons born in inferior castes rise into the Sathwic level and do good deeds. Brahmins of the type mentioned are only Janma Brahmins and not Karma Brahmins—Brahmins by birth and not Brahmins by virtue of their deeds. The others are low only by birth and not low at all by virtue of their deeds. The Vedas require co-ordination of birth and behaviour in castes.

Persons of pure Sathwic nature are rare in the world. They have mostly Rajas colouring and Sathwic character. Such individuals having attained noble birth are involved in Rajasic activities. They declare by their deeds that they are of mixed caste. The Vedas have not ignored such examples of mixed nature and the consequent effects on caste. The Vedas are impartial. They are not prejudiced against one and favourable to another. They do not elevate one set of persons or discard another, they only proclaim the truth that exists.

Let us consider an example. Kausika was a Kshatriya, that is to say, a person of Rajasic nature. However, as the result of his deeds in previous lives, Sathwic tendencies and attitudes entered his consciousness and he went about adhering strictly to truth. He transformed himself and sublimated his consciousness into a pure state. The manthra that he uttered, and which emanated from that level of consciousness is the Gayatri. He is known as Viswamitra, the *mitra* (friend) of the entire *Viswa,* for he became the well-wisher of the entire world! Brahmins have accepted and acclaimed that manthra as a Divine Gift. They have revered and recited it and derived immense Bliss. Kausika was therefore a Janma Kshatriya but he became a Karma-Brahmin and he was accepted as such by the Vedas, which emanated from the Voice of God. Thus it is clear that the Vedas proclaim the Path to all mankind without prejudice, partiality or sense of distinction. They pay attention only to the thoughts and acts of the individual.

About this, modern thinkers may have some doubt. This is quite natural. Let us see what that doubt is. When it is said that Divine Will has laid down the varnas, should they not exist in all lands? Surely, they should not be confined to this country, Bharath, they say. But there is no rule that whatever is created should necessarily be found to exist everywhere! It is not possible to realise that expectation.

It is but natural that restrictions and preferences concerning the process of living comprising the code have to be established with reference to each region, its atmosphere and climate, its peculiarities and specialties. There is no rule that trees that grow in Bharath should be found growing in other countries also. We cannot argue that stars which occupy the sky should exist also on the earth! There is no compulsion which insists that fishes that live in water should also live on hills.

God alone knows and decides what should happen to which, and where and why. All else are powerless. Events like birth are determined by circumstances of space, time, causation and the like. They are not bound by our needs or reactions, favourable or unfavourable. For this reason, mere observations and study of what is patent will only lead to confusing doubts about Varnas. Such doubts are inevitable for they are bred by the ego. The core of reality is separate and distinct from the fabrications of the ego. When people start acting according to the whims of fancy and speaking whatever comes to mind, we can only characterise them as models of sheer ignorance.

✧ ✧ ✧ ✧ ✧

18. Activity and Action

The countries of the world fall into two categories—Karma-bhoomi and *Bhoga-bhoomi*—countries where the people are devoted to activities with spiritual motivation and countries where the people pursue the pathways of the senses, with no higher purpose to guide them. The categories emphasise the ideals of the people, down the ages. Bharath or India is the Karma-bhoomi, where the people have discovered the proper goal of all activity, namely the glorification of God, resident within and without.

Karma is inevitable. It is immanent in every thought. It is of two kinds: Material and Spiritual, *Loukik* (connected with this world) and *Vaidik* (drawn from the Vedas or scriptural injunctions). Karma that merely sustains life is material. The Vaidik that elevates the human into the Divine is based on either the Vedas or on later texts like the Sastras or the Smrithi. They can be any of the three: mental, emotional or physical. They are also determined by the activities which the individual has adopted either in previous lives or in this. The consequences of acts done in past lives that are affecting this life are called *Praarabdha*. The Karma that one is engaged in now which is bound to affect the future is called *Aagaami*. The stored Karma that is slowly being worked out by the individual in life after life is called *Sanchitha*.

The Sruthi and the Smrithi texts of India have thus classified Karma, on the basis of the consequences it creates in the life of the individual. The word Karma is short and crisp. It is used freely by all and sundry. But the idea and ideals it conveys are of great significance to mankind. Karma is not simply physical; it is mental, verbal and manual. Each one can read into it as much value and validity as his reason can unravel.

Karma subsumes every activity of man—worldly, scriptural, the spiritual. All the three strands are, in truth, intertwined. The worldly Karma entails merit or demerit. The scriptural Karma is saturated with the experience of generations of good seekers. The spiritual devotes itself to the cleansing of the heart so that the indwelling God may be reflected therein. Karma is a stream that flows ever faster and faster turning the wheel of life and keeping it incessantly active.

Karma means movement, or that which urges the movement. Air moves in space. The moving air results in heat. It is the friction caused by aerial motion that makes the latent heat manifest. Living beings are able to maintain the temperature of the body, so long as air is breathed in and breathed out. The quicker the breath, the warmer the body. Warmth is the characteristic of fire. Fire is the origin of water. The Sun, as one can see, raises clouds. The particles of water get mixed with other elements and then, hardens into "earth" (ground, soil). The earth produces and fosters plants and trees, which feed and foster man and keep him hale and hearty. These plants give the grain that man lives upon, and the seminal fluid that produces progeny is the gift of the grain. Thus is the Karma of creation effected and continued. This is how the Smrithi summarises the process.

In short, Karma is observable here as movement, as progress, as evolution and as hereditary effect.

It is only natural and reasonable to expect that this vast flow, this constant movement must have something fixed and unmoving as base and support. This is exactly what is posited as Atma or Parabrahma. The very first vibratory movement on that base happened when Parabrahma became Parameswara and expressed the three thirsts for Jnana (Wisdom), *Iccha* (Wish) and *Kriya* (Will). That very movement was known as the primordial Karma, the Karma of Being, transforming itself into Becoming, the Karma of *Srshti* (creation).

It is the importance of Karma that necessitated the triple aspects of Divinity, Brahma (who causes creation), Vishnu (who supports and sustains) and Maheswara (who dissolves and destroys). It is the Law of Karma that rules the motion of the stars, the planets, the galaxies and other heavenly bodies in space. The same law directs and controls all that happens in all the worlds. It is inscrutable, in its very essence. No one can penetrate into the time or space when Karma was not. What, why, when and how events do happen is beyond the capacity of man to predict with accuracy. They are laid down from eternity to eternity.]

Just as a work being done or an activity which is engaging one, can be referred to as Karma, no work being done and no activity being engaged in, are also Karma! On seeing a person silent and calm, sitting quiet and doing nothing, we infer that he is free from activity. How, then, can he be described as doing Karma? What is meant by saying, "He is not doing any work." "He is not engaged in any activity"? That statement only means that "He is engaged in keeping himself away from any work or activity." So, it can be affirmed that men sometimes are busy doing work and sometimes busy with keeping work away from their attention. That is to say, they are engaged in Karma as well as *Akarma*. If he is not engrossed or attached with the Karma he does, and is engaged in it as his duty, as his way of worship; and if he is not attached to the fruit of his action, then he can practise Akarma even in Karma. This is the highest sadhana.

The very first act with which the career of a living being starts is "breathing and vibration of vital airs." When one thinks of it, it is wonderful how it happens. It is an amazing mystery. No human being resolves, at the moment of earthly life, to draw in and breathe out the air that exists around him. It proceeds without being willed or wished for. Not only man but every living organism is evidence of this great marvel. Doubts may be raised. "How can anything happen to man without his knowledge or without his resolution?" It is best to answer this doubt by confessing that man cannot unravel such secrets. Even if an attempt is made to reply that "Nature is the cause," the question still remains, "What exactly is Nature?" Breathing begins when life begins; it is an automatic, natural act—it is said. But all this is only saying the same thing in other words. They do not explain anything. It can as well be said that we are ignorant how it happens just when it is most essential. It is indeed surprising that the act of breathing is a mystery even to the person who breathes.

When we reflect on the fact that yogis exercise their will and stop their pulse-beats and their inhaling-exhaling process, we realise the power of Will in inducing Karma. Karma we can infer, is not something hanging loose in mid-air! Unless we become doers, deeds do not emanate. "*Na jaathi icchathi jethathe*," says the axiom in the *Nyayasastra*. "As one knows, so one wishes; as one wishes, so one acts." The Vedantha Sutras also proclaim the same truth. "*Yad dhyaathi, tad icchathi*" (That on which attention rests, that is the thing wished for). "*Yad icchatthi, tad karothi*" (That on which the wish rests, that is the thing for which deeds are done). "*Yad Karothi, tad bhavathi*" (That for which deeds are done, that is what becomes).

The manifest nature of the individual is moulded by desire. He shapes himself in line with his hopes, aspirations, attempts and achievements. Even his own future life is designed by him through his decisions and deeds. The force that his "reason" exerts on him and which directs his will in specific directions is known as Prakriti, or "Nature." When once it is discovered that one's own level of intelligence is the prime factor in determining one's inclinations and desires, then, it is easy to follow the means by which one can win release from the hold of "Prakriti."

Karma is generally known to mean "work." Transactions and actions of all kinds can be designated as "work." There are no levels of work like low or high. All work is holy if it has to be done for the upkeep and uplift of life. This is the reason why karma is praised as highly sacrosanct and desirable, and as fraught with meritorious or deleterious consequences.

The Hindus ascribe good fortune and bad, joy and sorrow, pleasure and pain, to the inescapable fruit of karma, and so it has happened that some have labelled as idlers those who do not resist and overwhelm distress, disease and pain. This is a partial paralytic view, which ignores the guiding principles and underlying philosophy of karma and knows it only as reflected in worldly, material activities. This view is adopted and emphasised to help particular sections to progress, that is all.

Take some examples from within your own experience. The commuter working in an office, the farmer who lives on his own toil, the porter who depends on his physical strength to gather the meagre means of livelihood, the blacksmith, the potter, the carpenter, the washerman, the barber—these are conscious of the activities which they have to follow and the sense of duty with which they have to follow them. They know that their lives cannot flow smoothly, when each one does not fill his assignment with dedication. Therefore, they engage themselves in their profession as best as their intelligence, skills and aspirations allow. But where is the need to prompt such people into further activity, to warn them and encourage them? We have to undertake this task only when they are unable or unwilling to carry on their duties.

In the case of Arjuna, who was confused about his duty and who withheld from battle since he was befogged by a feeling of renunciation, Sri Krishna said, "You have only to concentrate on the act and carry it out as you can. To act and only to act is the duty imposed on you." That was the immortal nectareous advice of the Lord. This advice is quoted by many. But it must be pointed out that this advice was given in the context of the restoration of righteousness. It deals with activities approved by holy scriptures and Sastras and not with worldly, sensual and animal activities like seeking food, shelter and mates.

Dharmaraja and others were immersed in worldly affairs and they were pastmasters in dealing with worldly situations. They were engaged constantly in following and fostering duties and responsibilities laid down for the four castes in society and the four stages of life. Why then should they be prompted and persuaded, counselled and commanded to *engage in battle*? Krishna advised only Arjuna to resume his bow and arrows, presenting before him many an argument. "You are born in the Kshatriya caste; that caste is entrusted by social norms with the execution of one social duty, fighting against injustice. Engaging in battle against wickedness is your responsibility. Do not desert that duty and discard that burden. Man is bound to the inclinations implanted in him by Nature. Again, consider this. Man has to be ever involved in some activity or other. He cannot live without it even for a moment. Therefore, it is best you act now, in accordance with the inclination and skill impressed on you by your ancestry and heredity." This is the lesson taught to him, the *Kula-Dharma*, the path of the caste or class to which he belonged.

Does "work" connote only acts by which food etc., are procured. Aircraft, ships, factories, hospitals are products of work. They too can be said to involve only worldly material "work." This type of work is important for living, and happy living here is a preparation for spiritual advancement in the hereafter. The more faulty one's activities in his worldly pursuits, the less success will be for the individual, the society and the nation. There can be no two opinions on these points. Nevertheless, men do not exert as efficiently and as enthusiastically for spiritual advancement, as they do for worldly success and fame. This is indeed a pity.

✧ ✧ ✧ ✧ ✧

19. Prayer

The relation between worldly and spiritual karmas has also to be examined. We plough the field deep and make it fit for the seeds to grow. We select good seeds and sow them in the furrows. We foster the saplings with care. We remove the weeds that hamper and harm them. We water the plants when they need. We protect the crop by the erection of fences. We keep vigilant watch and save the plants from pests. Take it that each of these crucial steps are carried out by us diligently and without delay, as and when required. But how can we be certain, in spite of all these, that the fruit of our labours will reach our homes and can be stored by us for our use? The irrigation canal might go dry any day. The sky might pour down too much rain or withhold it altogether. Pests might prove too powerful to be eliminated. They might destroy the crop just when harvest is in sight. But man should not, even when such disaster faces him, collapse, as if he has lost everything.

If one does not get rain in time for his crop, he can venture to fly into the clouds and scatter chemicals in order to induce showers, by artificial means. But what guarantee is there that the rain thus produced will fall on one's own land? Artificial means cannot affect the mood of gods. They help or hinder according to their will. When all paths are closed and when, at last, one decides to pray to God for rain; how is the prayer to be framed, in what form should it be uttered, these problems confront one. The disaster is evident. The only refuge is prayer—"Oh God! The growing crop in my field is fast drying up on account of unbearable thirst for rain. The canal has not even a drop of water to slake the thirst of men and cattle. Therefore, have pity on us. Give us rain, in plenty, soon."

Meanwhile, another problem has risen, let us say. One's neighbour has arranged for the celebration of some festival and since rain will ruin the festival he has planned, and cause great inconvenience to the participants, he prays equally fervently, "Oh God, keep off the rains until this celebration is over."

Both these applicants are intense devotees of God, the one who clamours for rain and the one who opposes the rain. What is God to do, under these conditions? Whose prayer is He to fulfil? Of course, answering prayers saturated with sincerity is the characteristic of the Divine. When the prayers of devotees clash, how is He to shape His Grace? God is free, His Will is Law. But He is bound in some sense by His own Love and Compassion.

The monarch of a realm cannot satisfy the desire of every one of his subjects. He cannot claim the power of fulfilling all their needs. Why? He is unable to fulfil for himself all that he desires. If he attempts to satisfy every wish that arises in him, the subjects are certain to rise up against him and pull him down from the seat of power. There is that danger always dangling over him. Because, however mighty the monarch, he has to obey certain rules and honour some limitations laid down to ensure a just rule. These might have been laid down by the very monarch; but once promulgated, he too is bound by them and had to honour them. If he casts them aside or transcends them or oversteps them, chaos will be the consequence. For, the subjects too will exercise their freedom to cast them aside or override them. "As the King, so the subjects." "*Yatha raja, thatha praja*."

The person who is the author of the law must himself obey the law. He cannot stay away. The monarch must always hold as his ideal the welfare and happiness of his subjects Their welfare and happiness are essential for his own welfare and happiness. They are so closely interrelated.

To satisfy the proper and praiseworthy desires of his subjects is the inescapable duty of the monarch. It is for this reason that the monarch, in order to carry out his duties effectively and smoothly, has assigned the task to many subordinate authorities, instead of himself attending to all matters concerning the kingdom and the subjects.

The rulers of worldly states have perforce to lay down hard and fast limitations and conditions, disciplines and duties in order to ensure welfare, prosperity and progress. Imagine then how many more such have to be imposed by the Lord who holds Himself responsible for the entire Cosmos! For the smooth and safe working of the various facets of Nature, He has to prescribe flawless rules. Just contemplate how numerous and universal they have to be! These affect every activity and inactivity in nature. Each unit must have (and has) its own peculiar restrictions and regulations. It is more or less, itself, within the larger framework. It has a separate Head with limbs of government, co-ordinating duties and responsibilities and co-operating with others.

The prayers of the afflicted for timely help or useful guidance are attended to by the appropriate units only. Therefore, if through ignorance or want of care, the pleading is addressed to the wrong Head, what can he do? He can only cast it aside, remarking that it does not concern Him since it has been wrongly addressed to Him. So, prayers for specific benefits and bounties have to be directed to the departments with which they are related. The divinity concerned with rain is Varuna. So, prayers for rain or about rain have to be directed to Him, for, He alone is authorised to deal with such. Similarly, Surya is the Head of the Realms of Health and Splendour. Ganapathi is the Head of the department that deals with prevention of difficulties that hamper good works. Bhudevi is the goddess in charge of vegetation. Cultivated crops and medicinal plants are fostered by Chandra. Thus, each group of Divine manifestations and expressions has a lesser divine authority empowered to supervise and manage it. They are referred to as Deities. There are Deities supervising, guarding and guiding each one of the senses of man.

It may be asked, "God is One. Why then can He not listen to and fulfil our prayers Himself?" This question is based on a mistake, it is a sign of weakened faith. Of course, there is only one God. But in the governance of the Cosmos, there must needs be different fields of activity to rule and regulate. These have subordinate deities. If you write a letter to me and address it to another, it will reach only the addressee! It cannot be *presented* before the person whom you desire to approach. So too, you have to address the Deity in charge, concerned with the fulfilment or denial of the desire you have entertained. Then, that Deity would interest himself in your problem and initiate whatever steps he can to solve it.

It is essential to inquire into the credentials one has before one formulates the prayer. That inquiry will reveal whether one's thoughts and resolutions, hopes and desires arise from firm Faith or not. How to test and discover the truth? People take a piece of gold and draw with it a line on a slice of stone. Then they examine that streak and assess the quality. The test which will reveal the quality of your Faith is whether you are practising sincerely the injunctions laid down by God. Your beliefs and actions must be expressions of Faith. They must have holiness as their core. They must be so full of love and compassion that they attract on you the Grace of God.

Activity emanating from such sacred belief and faith is the goal of the Karma segment of Vedic scriptures. It is the tap root of human progress. It is the very breath of happy human existence. It is the food that can alone allay the hunger of man. It is the life-sustaining water that can cure his thirst. Activity or Karma is as essentially bound with man as his need to discover and realise his own Reality. Therefore, the first and continuing duty of man is to engage himself in activities that are taught in the Vedas, or approved therein.

Three types of activity reach God and earn His Grace: (1) activity not prompted by personal desire, (2) activity emanating from unselfish Love and (3) prayer arising from pure hearts. These are the items to which the Lord pays heed. They reach God direct. The rest are the concern of deities who preside over their disposal. Therefore, prayers have to be unselfish, saturated with Love, and free from the taint of "attachment to the gift that the prayer would bring."

The word Sastra that is frequently used to indicate scriptures means "that which commands, orders, directs with authority." "Before eating food, cook it well. Before sowing seeds, prepare the soil through ploughing"—the Sastras need not contain such orders. Who commands and where is that command laid down that the new-born calf shall seek food at the udder of the mother cow where it is already stored to appease its hunger pangs? Birth takes place along with sustenance for the being born.

As a matter of fact, the sustenance is ready first and the birth of the individual to be sustained takes place later. The individual's food and standard of living are dependent on the merit or demerit accumulated in previous lives while struggling for these two. He uses his intelligence to overcome the obstacles and cultivate the skills needed to succeed in this struggle. But the really valuable guidelines for human progress are beyond the understanding of man and even the capacities of his intelligence. Nevertheless, the characteristics of his conduct and behaviour, his attitudes and aptitudes are delineated in the Vedas, and demarcated in the Sastras. Activity is as essential on Vedic and Sastric lines as they are for humans in the worldly level. The learned should realise that activities recommended in the scriptures promote the best interests of man here and lead to peace and harmony in the hereafter.

In the art of beneficial activity, the goal of "Service to mankind" occupies the foremost place. Of course, the individual pursuing the goal is also a beneficiary, since he is part of the living community which he serves. He is the co-sharer in the magnificent adventure. Knowing this and being aware of this truth when engaged in the service are themselves the highest urges for service.

Today, we hear everywhere, slogans like, "*Manava seva is Madhava seva*" (Service to man is service to God), "*Loka seva is Lokesa seva*" (Service to the world is the service rendered to the Lord of the universe), "*Jana seva is Janardhana seva*" (Service to the people is the service to the Lord of the people), "*Jiva seva is Deva seva*" (Service to the embodied is the service to the Divine)—each one highlighting the idea that the service rendered to man is worship offered to God. This idea is very true, and very valid. But the method of service is not being well-thought out by many. The call for service to mankind is heard and welcomed. But how and where that service is to be practised is not reasoned out and decided. Each one follows his own inclination and impulse. The most powerful impulse is self-aggrandisement, which is camouflaged as service. In the name of "service," neither worldly prosperity nor spiritual advance is furthered. More destruction than construction is achieved. Helping one, co-operating with another, sympathising with others when they suffer defeat, disease or distress—all these must cater not merely for the individual, but also for the harmony and happiness of the world.

The organisation of the urge to serve and the directions into which these were channelled had prevailed since ages as laid down by the sages who were the forefathers. The forefathers believed that the very observance of Dharma (righteousness and justice) by the individual contributed to the welfare of the world and could be evaluated as "service." The broad circular heavy footprint of the elephant can include and even obliterate the footprints of many an animal. So too, the imprint of Dharma includes service to society and to mankind. This was the faith of the Sages.

High ideals are inspired by Dharma. The forefathers imbibed them along with the breast milk of their mothers. Therefore, their practice of Dharma was pure, praiseworthy and productive of the highest good. It was believed in those ancient days that the festive feeding of the hungry, provision of houses for those without shelter, the construction of temples, the digging of tanks and wells, were all conducive to the happiness of man. Good men who propagated such ideals were discovered and gathered, fostered and fended. Entire villages were earmarked for them and cultivable land allotted for their upkeep. The cool comforting moonlight of the fame of these leaders and guides has lasted even unto this day, providing unshakeable examples of love, compassion and wisdom in the service of humanity.

✧ ✧ ✧ ✧ ✧

20. The Primal Purpose

The very first step to ensure peace and harmony to mankind is for each one observing the Dharma or code of conduct laid down for him in his own religion. If one holds his own faith and its essential principles mandatory, one can serve himself best and also serve others well. Dharma in this context means action in accordance with the traditions of the culture of the land. In every facet of the Dharma of this country, the ideal of world peace and world prosperity is immanent.

"*Athaatho Karma Jijnaasa*." "Now, for the inquiry into Activity"—thus begins the intellectual probe into the mystery of Karma, which in our scriptures extends over vast fields. For example, to give away in charity and as gift is a very proper type of Karma. But one must be aware that egoism can pollute it and make it improper. It is laid down that plentiful charity now will ensure happiness in a future life, so that consideration of this advantage for oneself might well lead men to good karma. Even if many have no eye on the future, it can be asserted that most charity flows from egoistic motives. This is an all-too-evident fact.

People feel proud that they have helped others. They are eager to be praised as beneficent and munificent. This attitude reveals their ignorance, Ajnana. It springs from non-awareness of actuality, Maya. In the Vedas and Sastras, the Rishis while elaborating on do's and don'ts, stress non-violence, compassion, service to the world, charity, etc. as virtues to be acquired. Saint Vidyaranya named these as the very essence of Indian Wisdom.

Wisdom is the precious ambrosia gathered from all sources of knowledge and all the arts of earning it. It is the sweet, sustaining butter churned and collected from the Sastras. Wisdom is not to be defined as the capacity to discriminate and declare, "this is flat" or "this is round," or "this is a hill," "this is a house," or "this is a thorn." That is the common belief. This is only knowledge. Next, we have what may be called good knowledge (*Sujnana*); when man is able to distinguish between right and wrong or good and bad, when he can discover, "This activity is for my betterment and the betterment of others." Both Jnana and Sujnana are confined to the intellect of man. There is a higher stage called *Vijnana*, when the heart is transformed by loyalty to Truth, non-violence, and compassion. Such a person can understand himself, his kinship with the Cosmos, and with the Creator of the Cosmos. He lives in accordance with that understanding, without doubt or disharmony. Ajnana or ignorance breeds sorrow. Vijnana confers joy. If one hesitates to call any experience Vijnana, let him examine whether it is material or spiritual, on the touchstone, "Does it give me unalloyed joy?" and then classify it as such. The yardstick for Vijnana is Dharma. The more Dharma is put into practice, the more one gets rooted in Vijnana.

Action through Vijnana is evidenced by the peace and prosperity of the nation. The decline of Dharma reveals the disappearance of Vijnana. Eras are differentiated on the basis of adherence or aversion to Dharma. When Dharma, justice and harmony prevail fully and fearlessly, it is said to walk securely over the land on four legs. The times when it is so observed are also referred to as Kritha Yuga, the Kritha Era. When justice and harmony prevail less and less, people feel that Dharma has to limp its way on three legs! The times suffering from this handicap are referred to as the Thretha Era, the Thretha Yuga. When justice and harmony prevail only a quarter as much as in the Kritha Yuga, Dharma has to struggle on two legs. That is the Dwapara Yuga. When they have no respect paid to them and when they are largely non-existent, Dharma stands on one leg, as it were. This is the Kali Yuga, we are told by the scriptures.

The wisdom of the Bharathiyas is nourished by Dharma. Though Indian thought asserts that "the objective world" is basically untrue and though it teaches us that our involvement with life and its problems is an illusive adventure that cannot affect our Reality, the Sastras, which are the roots of that thought, do not advise us to discard Dharma. For, to grasp the Highest and the Ultimate Truth, Dharma is indispensable. The four traditional goals of human endeavour (the *Purusharthas*: Dharma, Artha, Kama and Moksha) are laid down to cater to those who live in the belief that the objective world is "True."

It can be seen that even among the four goals, Dharma has been placed first and foremost. The state to be earned by the first three achievements is Moksha, which is mentioned last. The person who seeks riches and the fulfilment of his desires along the path laid down by Dharma can alone win victory. That way lies liberation which gives man the highest bliss.

Nevertheless, since the Jivi or the individualised, limited self is caught in the net of desire or Kama, the goals of Dharma and Moksha do not enter its vision or arouse any interest. It takes delight in sinking and floating on the waves of material pleasures (Artha and Kama). This is nothing strange in persons of that nature.

The search for food, the avoidance of fear and the enjoyment of sloth and sleep—in these, man and animal are equally eager and equally involved. The search for Moksha and the observance of Dharma—these promote man to a level of existence higher than the animal level. If that yearning is absent, man cannot claim to be human.

India is acclaimed by her own people as well as by people of other countries for holding forth the ideal of Vijnana, the highest wisdom. Here, there is faith that God exists in all lands. Here there is constant effort to discriminate between Dharma and what is not Dharma. Value is attached to justice and virtue. Compassion towards living beings and non-violence are also held high as guides to conduct. Efforts are made to distinguish truth and untruth. Temples still flourish and are still replete with spiritual vibrations. We have in other countries many Houses of God constructed by man such as churches and mosques but they are not so ancient and charged so long and so deep with Divinity.

All religions are One, declares this land of Bharath. There may be difference in the number and nature of the limbs; the message each conveys is the same as all the rest. This is the discovery of India, and her announcement to mankind.

For directing their prayers to God, one person has, as his symbol, a stone; another has a piece of metal; a third uses wood. But all attach great importance to prayer and believe in its beneficent effects. One person turns to the East, while praying. Another regards the West as really sacred. The prayer of both concerns the same wants and inadequacies. This is the conclusion arrived at by Bharathiya sages and thinkers. Each faith has its own Scriptures and doctrines. But one must pay attention to the special features too. For example, God is so intimately felt as one's own;

that prayers are often addressed to God in singular: "Can you not do this?" or "Are you incapable of protecting me?" or "Have you become weak of hearing?" This is a peculiar trait among Bharathiyas.

However a person feels or thinks, he transforms himself into the embodiment of those feelings and thoughts. If he is immersed in the truth that he is God, he can become Divine. However, if he is immersed in the falsehood that he is the King of the Land, he will be deemed mad or traitorous. He might even be beheaded for treason. God will not treat you as insane or insubordinate. Every being is Divine. This is the final judgement of the wisdom of Bharath.

Logic and intellectual investigation can give only partial accounts of the Truth. Everything in creation has many phases and many angles. Reason can observe only from one angle; it can see only one phase. The intellect that has been purified and clarified through the activities (Karma) laid down in the Vedas can succeed in observing both phases. Without undergoing the process of purification and clarification, Reason can work only within the bounds of the materialist world. So, the conclusions that it presents before us can only be partially true. But the intellect subjected to the processes of cleansing and sharpening in the Vedic way can serve us by presenting a picture of the full Truth of the objective world. Most of the other Faiths rely on principles reached by reason, not subjected to these disciplines taught by the Vedas. Bharathiyas have the Sastras which illumine far beyond the bounds and limits of the temporary and the temporal.

The Universe is the Macrocosmos. The Individual Being is the Microcosmos. The first is the *Brahmanda*, the second is the *Pindanda* (Physical Universe). But the basic Truth of both is One, the same. That One is independent and unrelated to any other fact or thing. When That is realised in this manner, it can be called Brahmam. When it enters the awareness as the Universe, it is referred to as Parabrahmam. The basic truth of the Universe is Atma. The basic Truth of the Individual is also Atma. All that appear as different from Atma are of the region of "delusion" or Mithya. Mithya or delusion implies a condition which until inquiry appears real but on inquiry is known to be unreal. It is only an appearance, this universe and its supposed basis—an appearance caused by Ignorance or Maya. The power that deludes us into believing that the created cosmos is true and real is also an emanation from the Atma. When this power operates and the Atma is clothed with it, it is referred to as Paramatma.

Atma is the *Satchitananda* or *Sath-Chith-Ananda*, treated as one inseparable composite. Maya too is a composite of the three gunas or natural modes or qualities—Thamasic, Rajasic and Sathwic. They express themselves in *Ichha Sakthi* (Desire), *Kriya Sakthi* (Deed) and *Jnana Sakthi* (Wisdom). The quality called Thamas creates the appearance of diversity, hiding the basic ONE and Only. The quality named Rajas explores the Truth and the pleasures of wisdom. The quality named Sathwa is a clear mirror, it gives a correct picture of things and events that happen before it. It reflects Parabrahmam and reveals Easwara or God. God thus manifested becomes the Universe or Jagat created by His Will. The reflected Easwara does not have the capacity of Maya or Delusion. As the clear water of a lake has froth and bubbles on the surface, the Atma's essential nature seems to be tarnished by the deluding appearance of Maya and its product—the Jagath or Universe, with varied Names and Forms. When the three modes of Maya are in balance and in a state of unruffled equipoise, the Universe is termed unmanifest, Avyaktha. This is termed the "seed-state" since all subsequent variations are subsumed and latent in it. When Thamas and Rajas have their impact, Creation is caused and the Cosmos comes about. They agitate living beings into activity. The deluding force is conditioned by the three modes, as and when each expresses itself and asserts its influence over the rest. When Sathwa predominates, it is named as Atmamaya; when Rajas is ascendant, it becomes Avidya or Non-knowledge and when Thamas holds sway, it becomes *Thaamasi* or dullness. When the Atma is reflected in the Sathwic mode, the image becomes Easwara; when reflected in Rajas, it becomes Jiva or individual Being; and when reflected in Thamas, it becomes Matter. It is the mould, the upadhi, that causes the distinction between Easwara (God), Jiva (the living being) and *Dravya* (matter); when there is no upadhi or mould or case, all these are Atma. Since the Universe is God, Jiva and Matter, it can be truly described as the composite of the three modes. The Universe has manifested, in order to serve the highest interests of living beings and of man, the most intelligent of them all. While affirming that the Atma is reflected in the Sathwic, Rajasic and Thamasic modes, producing impressions of Easwara, the Individual and Matter, one point has to be emphasised. The mirror that conditions the image has only limited capacity. It can reflect only objects that are opposite to it. But when the mirror is either convex or concave in surface or when its plain surface is soiled with dirt, the image will suffer contortion or fail in clarity. This, however, does not affect the object; only the image is distorted or defaced. But the object itself is usually condemned on the basis of its reflection or image.

Brahmam too appears distorted on account of Maya and Ajnana (ignorance) and this distortion which is a superimposed characteristic is supposed wrongly to adhere to Brahmam itself! The image of Parameswara (the Supreme Godhead) is also a reflection in the Maya mirror. As milk turns into curds, Brahmam has turned into Jagath or Universe. This transformation is the handiwork of Maya. Brahmam is the Master of Maya and not its subordinate. It releases the Maya Power and directs it. So, the personalised Brahmam or Parameswara is known as Omnipotent and Omniscient. The Jiva, the Easwara and the *Bhootha* (elements or matter)—these three contribute to the progress of the individual, each in its own way.

The Easwara or Lord is the fulfilment of all desires. All objects of enjoyment in the Universe emanate from His

Will, and so He has no desire at all. He has manifested the Universe not for the realisation of any desire of His or filling any vacuity He suffered from, but for the benefit entirely of living beings. "*Na me, Partha asthi Karthavyam, Thrishu Lokeshu Kinchana*—there is no duty binding on me, Partha, in the three worlds," says Krishna. Creation, manifestation, or emanation is His very nature. Hence, the description (*Leela Vinodi*) "Revelling in play," is often ascribed to Him. It is His Willpower that is filling all living beings with consciousness and helping them to be alert and active. He grants to each the consequence of thought, word and deed and is therefore described as the Giver-of-the-fruit-of-Activity (*Karma phala-pradaatha*). Without the intercession of the Lord, activity cannot result in consequence; nor can certainty arise that a particular act will result in an identifiable manner. Besides, the sages declare that Karma (activity) is momentary. The thought arises and the act is done. The act is followed by the fruit. It is not possible to predict when the fruit will be available or what its nature will be. Hence, we have to admit that it all depends on the Lord's Command. What cannot be interpreted by our limited intellect has to be ascribed to His Command.

However long the interval, however many lives elapse, one cannot escape the obligation of suffering from the consequences of one's actions. There can be no place for inquiry into the origins of the act or when it happened, for, one has to trace from the beginning of Time itself. One cannot discover the beginnings of the Lord, the Universe, the Living Being, Activity and Ignorance; they are all beyond the Beginning. In the *Bhagavad Gita*, Krishna declares, "*Gahanaa Karmano Gathih*" (the way of action is elusively subtle and difficult to discover). The consequence might confront the person, even after the passage of many lives. The Lord is the eternal Witness, the Power that presides over every act. Looked at from this point of view, one has to realise and declare that the Lord and the Individual are bound inextricably together. In the absence of living beings, there can be no Lord. When there are no children, how can the word "father" be meaningful? So the Lord, it can be said, manifested the Universe, in order to provide living beings with fields of activity and in order to grant them the consequences of those actions. The five elements serve the same purpose. They also help constitute the physical vehicles of life, in accordance with the quality and quantity of those consequences. There are also regions called *Lokas* where beings which have accumulated great merit or gathered terrible sins have to be in the hereafter. These have no relation to the regions or bodies that are visible to us.

Life-principle and Individual-principle do both mean the same. Both indicate that they have emerged from absence of the awareness of the Truth, or Avidya. This again is due to bondage to the Gunas or tendencies. The individual is marked by the presence of *Rajo Guna* or the active work-prone passionate mode, though it has the seeds of the other two modes also in its makeup. The Jagath or creation itself has its origin when the Truth veiled itself in Avidya or delusion. The modes manifested at that same moment and individuals differentiated according to the predominance of one or the other of the three chief modes, caused by the total effect of the Karmas gone through in life after life. When he is endowed more with the Sathwic mode, he becomes a Bhagavatha, inspired by devotion to God and engaged mostly in adoring and praising Divine Glory. Preponderance of Rajasic traits renders him a strong intelligent man, content to be a man with no higher aspirations toward Divinity. If he is ruled by the *Thamasic Guna*, he becomes as bound to the body and its needs as birds and beasts.

The Jivi (living being) on account of an intellect caught in the coils of delusion imagines that it is an "effect" and so bound to some "cause." This non-awareness of Truth has to be conquered by Atma Vidya which urges towards this adventure and ensures success. It will destroy the distinction, now believed in, between Jiva and Jagath (the subject and the object, man and the Cosmos). To help man in this heroic duel, and to make him aware of the Truth, the Vedas prescribe Karmas or desirable activities in what is referred to as *Karma Kanda*. So long as one is caught in avidya, man and cosmos, the upper and lower worlds, dharma and adharma, karma, bhakthi and jnana—these concepts have to be respected and one's life shaped accordingly. So long as one is established in the validity of the "diversity" apparent in the Universe, one acts according to the limits imposed by the personalised God, the Easwara.

The Universe is for each Jivi its own mental picture and nothing else, fundamentally. So, unless one unravels the mind and its processes, the Brahma principle is difficult to understand. Those who have not understood the real nature of the sky will mistake it as a dome of smoke and dust. So too, the Atma is mistaken, through non-awareness of reality, to be enclosed in and embodied as intellect or Buddhi, to be involved in activity and enjoyment of the results of activity, to be caught up in the twin bonds of joy and sorrow, and to be embroiled in happiness and misery and also in bondage and liberation. From the angle of change (*Vyavahara*), the higher Truth will naturally appear as different, though they are inextricably interrelated. Space is one. But as a result of the diversity of vessels, it seems to be enclosed in the home, the pot, the building and the canvas. There is no truth in this sectionalised existence; it is the One space that exists in all these "containers"—houses, lakes, hills, etc.—which are shapes and forms, with distinct names attached to them and different modes of behaviour and use. So too, individual beings (Jivas) have different names and forms, peculiarities and specialities of use and behaviour. But like the string that holds the beads, passing in and through each and holding them together, the Superconsciousness in all individuals is ONE.

That is the Atma, which is mistaken as I, through ignorance. As long as this truth is not won, man cannot release himself from the hold of multiplicity and change. The scriptures communicate to us this Reality and exhort us to realise it. What is it that, if known, everything else can be known? When the Atma is known, declare the scriptures (Sruthi), everything can be known. The Jagath (the Cosmos) is only relatively real. It is partly false. Knowing it is unprofitable and unnecessary. It is not a legitimate purpose of Life. Life is best spent and human effort best directed when awareness of the Atma principle is sought to be attained. The Sruthi warns man against other vain pursuits. The Sruthi texts and allied sacred literature like Smrithis, Ithihasas and Puranas do not teach us anywhere how the Cosmos was created or advise us to study and understand the origins and the process. They do not declare the absence of that knowledge as calamitous. They even assert that the task is impossible.

"Why worry how the Cosmos was born or when it will die? Worry rather about yourself." That is the lesson emphasised by the scriptures. "Know Thyself." Once you know yourself, everything else will be automatically clear. You are a *Pindanda* (Physical universe composed of elements) in the Brahmanda, a microcosm in the macrocosm. Just as the knowledge of one single claypot is enough to know all about clay pots, when you know your self, all else can be known.

In order to persuade a child to stop weeping and regain joy, the *Ayah* (nurse) relates a fairy tale which pleases it. The Ayah's sole purpose is to calm the child. The fairy tale is only a means modelled on its intellectual level. In the same manner, the Jivi, fascinated by the beginningless attraction of maya and bound by tendencies cultivated during many lives in the past, cannot avoid inquiring into the origins of the Universe which he encounters. The Sruthi answers such inquiry in words that give temporary relief. For, the question, how was the Universe created, is on a par with the question, how is a dream created? The dream originates from sleep or *Nidra*; the Universe originates through illusion or Maya. Just as the dream has no order or law, the Universe also is too full of mystery and Maya. There is only ONE, not two as often happens in a dream. This is the doctrine of Adwaitha. Very much like the question of the origin of creation, another problem that generally worries man is, how did this ignorance happen? The solution has been provided by the sage-preceptor, Vasishta, to Sri Ramachandra. "Rama!" he said, "Rather than entangling yourselves in the inquiry regarding how Ignorance entered Man, I would exhort you to be engaged in efforts to get rid of it." This lesson is directed not only to Rama but to all mankind. It helps all who do not possess the realisation of the Truth behind the objective world. Ajnana or ignorance is the name given to ignoring what is one's own inner experience—that the universe is an ever-changing phenomenon.

Why then are we troubled by this question? Be convinced that you have this ignorance, give up the struggle to get rid of attachment to this changing world with its concomitant birth-death cycle. It is only another evidence of this ignorance to argue whether this Ajnana adheres to

Brahmam or emanates from the Jivi. Surely it is much more essential to concentrate on the methods by which the ignorance can be discarded. For it will certainly yield to wisdom or Jnana. Jnana is Light. Ignorance is darkness. Darkness can persist Only until Light shines.

21. The Inner Inquiry

"All this will disappear and lose individuality with the emergence of Jnana, the Highest Wisdom," said the Sage Vasishta to Rama. "Rama," he advised, "You have to understand how this non-knowledge grew and by what means it can be destroyed."

There is one mystery hidden in this advice. Centuries of inquiry have failed to unravel the secret—wherefrom did the Cosmos originate? How did it emerge? If It had a Personal Cause, the inquiry could have succeeded. The Cosmos or Jagath is not such an object. The questions "How did It emerge?" "Wherefrom did It originate?" are exactly on a par with the question, "How did the "serpent" appear on the "rope" and cause the "terror"? Only the rope exists there; the serpent was imposed thereon, during dusk, by the defective intellect of the onlooker. That is to say, on account of the illusion created by reasoning. In other words, ignorance is the basis of the misapprehension.

Brahmam is the "rope"; Jagath is the "serpent" superimposed on it by Reason afflicted by illusion. We cognise Brahmam as Jagath; we take one thing as another, so long as this affliction holds sway. Therefore, it is best to conclude that the Jagath is an object which originated in our own Buddhi (Intellect) and emerged out of the same faulty faculty. An object born of such a delusion and confirmed by only an infirm intellect can never be true. When the delusion goes, when the infirmity disappears, the Jagath so caused also disappears.

"*Aham Ajnah*" "I am ignorant." Everyone has to acknowledge to himself this fact about himself. He cannot escape making this declaration about himself. The conclusion set forth in all sacred texts and scriptures is that all this is Brahmam. Setting this aside, if the individual still claims that he is "I," he is asserting that he is but an Ajnani, or ignoramus.

A doubt may arise, whether it is at all possible to forget oneself and believe that one is something else. We have already seen that the acceptance of Mithya (truth polluted with untruth) is the sign of the ignorant person. In the dusk, falsehood is superimposed on truth. The serpent is visualised on the rope lying on the road. The delusion affects the consciousness and warps the Buddhi, so that they forget their genuine nature which is ananda or ecstatic delight. They impose on themselves the limitations of individuality and consider themselves as Jivis. They welcome the belief that happiness is outside them in the objective world and they entangle themselves in samsar, the moving, changing, restless world. They suffer the twin blows of fate and fortune. Such persons are taught by the Sruthi, by the Vedas and sacred texts, to transform their lives through consistent endeavour for knowing and realising the Atma.

The protagonists of Adwaitha are not engaged in proving that there is something named ignorance or Ajnana. "I am not happy. I have no joy. I want this. I must earn this," such longings constitute the Individual or the Jivi. This attitude is the core of the ignorance. So, if you seek to destroy the ignorance that separates and stultifies, this attitude must be transformed and the conviction that "I am the embodiment of happiness, I am the One who has realised Desire" has to be cultivated. The person who has the former attitude has got *Jivathwa Buddhi*, individualised knowledge, and he who has the latter knowledge has Jnana or Universalised Wisdom. Bearing the burden of non-existent problems, kicking up dust in the confusion, tied helplessly to the wheel of birth and death, man curses himself in despair. The Adwaithic Texts arose in order to warn man against this Ajnana and to arouse in him the Jnana that can save him from misery and wrong. Truly speaking we are Ajnana, so long as we feel we are in bondage. In fact, we have not been created. We are not limited or abridged or bound. The faith that has taken root, namely, "There is a Jagath which contains me along with other similar seekers of happiness, in that search, I meet joy and grief, and encounter birth and death"—this is the fundamental Ajnana.

"We become what our thoughts are." These thoughts on the validity of the objective world and the value of the joys derivable therefrom, though they emanate from Ajnana, do shape us from within. The reason why we are caught in this mould lies in the absence of four requisites: (1) attention towards *Adhyatmic* gain (spiritual progress); (2) steady faith; (3) devotion and (4) the grace of God. Even if one of these four is absent, man cannot experience the highest Bliss of the Absolute.

Our inquiry should not be directed to the obvious and the superficial. This line of inquiry will only mislead us into believing what is not the Cosmos. It makes us forget that it is our mind that has generated this panorama of cosmic proportions and presented it to us as Truth.

It is indeed strange that this huge Cosmos depends ultimately on whether "I" cognise it as such or not! "If you feel it is there, it is there. If you feel it is not there, it is not there!" This means that we have to go deep into this process of the mind of man. Is there any occasion when our assertion leads to the existence of a thing and our negation results in its disappearance? Or is this conclusion a figment of the imagination?

Inquiry on these lines would undoubtedly reveal the Truth. When the rope is seen in darkness, by mistake, by ignorance, the serpent arises and appears in its place, displacing the truth of the rope. For some reason, when the truth is known, and the onlooker feels, "This is no serpent. It is a rope," the serpent disappears, for it was mere "falsehood." So feeling or thinking is able to create the serpent and also to destroy it. Assertion creates, negation destroys. Both are mental processes which can be classified as "thoughts."

Though there are diverse levels and grades, all these are but thoughts. Where do these thoughts emerge from? Are they free to emerge spontaneously? To this question, the answer is: "*Buddhi Karma Anusaarini.*" "Our intellect follows the lead of our activities. Thoughts arise in conformity with the attachment one develops and the results one anticipates from one's actions." The very first motive for action is, "I must attain happiness and harmony." This motive arises from the ignorant assumption that the world is real.

Education sans wisdom, mere wisdom bereft of discrimination, action without discretion, erudition lacking sagacity, power not justified by credentials, statements not based on truth, music wanting in melody, adoration not sustained by devotion, a person devoid of common sense and character, a student not endowed with humility and a discourse that fails to inspire: these serve no useful purpose.

In addition to knowledge derived from the sacred texts, one should gain wisdom through experience. Knowledge without personal experience is futile. Wisdom lodged within us will be of no avail if it is static. It will only assume the form of mere scholarship. If such learning is brought within the ambit of practice it is creditable. Acquiring and hoarding of wealth will be of no avail if it is not consecrated and spent for the welfare of the world. Similarly mere acquisition of knowledge from books is a futile exercise. Knowledge becomes blessed only when it is translated into actions which promote the good of humanity. This translation of knowledge into experience is possible only when one passes through the three stages of Knowing (*Jnatum*), Visualising (*Drashtum*) and Entering (*Praveshtum*).

First, one must learn about the precious truths contained in the sacred texts from veterans in the field. When you learn about them you naturally take an interest in them. Then you develop an urge to visualise those truths at any cost. This is the first stage of Knowing.

In the second stage, you carefully peruse, examine and collect such sacred texts wherever they may be available. You read and directly visualise them. With great perseverance you inquire, comprehend and enjoy them. Thus you derive some satisfaction that you have discerned certain profound truths. This is the second stage of Visualising.

It is not enough if you make progress in the first two stages. You must experience what is known and seen. By entering the arena of experience, one should feel complete identification with the Ideal. If one lies down after having consumed food, it will cause indigestion. However, if one consumes daily the requisite quantity of food and undertakes some physical work it will be digested, and converted into blood, will offer nourishment. In the same manner, we should translate into experience and action what we have known and seen, by assimilating it and utilising it for the progress of our country as well as for the welfare of humanity.

It is easy to memorise passages from books and deliver lectures. Knowledge acquired merely through the reading of books is bookish knowledge. This is quite an ordinary type of knowledge. What has been heard, seen and understood should be put into practice at least to some extent. This is the stage of Entering.

The ancient sacred lore contain several precious truths. Invaluable gems lie hidden in them. Many scientific theories relating to the atom are also to be found there. Students should seek to unravel these hidden truths and harness them to the effort for human welfare. There must be the urge as well as the determination in them to explore undiscovered truths. They should not rest content with delivering discourses and appearing on forums of discussion.

Only those possessing a genuine spirit of inquiry can disseminate real knowledge in the world. Mere superficial knowledge will be of no avail. There is no knowledge that can surpass the knowledge derived from direct experience. It must be acquired through self-effort, initiative, determination and perseverance. It should be utilised for technological development and the increase of production, which makes for the country's progress.

It is necessary to derive wisdom from experience, but it is equally essential to develop the faculty of discrimination which enables us to employ it for the well-being of the country. Education without discrimination, and wisdom without discernment are of no use. Education is one thing and discrimination is quite another. Discrimination is the faculty that enables us to distinguish good from bad and confers upon us the ability to decide how much importance is to be given to various aspects in a given situation. Discrimination is a component of wisdom. Without discrimination one cannot pursue the right path. It is a mark of sagacity to display discrimination in all actions. Through researches in atomic energy one may invent destructive weapons which can reduce to ashes the entire world in a second. The same atomic energy might help us to generate millions of kilowatts of electric power which could be utilised for industries and agriculture, transforming the country into a smiling garden. An educated person should display discrimination in such matters and take the right course of action. Man's discoveries and inventions should not be for evil purposes which lead to disaster and destruction. Discrimination guides us in properly employing them for augmenting production and promoting human welfare.

A man endowed with wisdom and discrimination will be honoured and adored even though he may not have wealth or position. A person devoid of wisdom and discrimination can never blossom spiritually even though he may be an eminent educationist, a prominent scientist or a multimillionaire. One without wisdom and discrimination cannot even distinguish between *dharma* and *adharma*. Therefore, every student must acquire wisdom and discrimination without resting on his oars after gaining theoretical knowledge. He should develop farsighted vision along with wisdom and use it for the uplift of society.

In addition to wisdom, discrimination and experience, one should also possess inspiring common sense. It cannot be acquired through books. In order to gain it one must travel extensively. It is for this purpose that our ancestors went on pilgrimages to see, speak to and touch the feet of holy men in sacred places. They also saw many sights and objects in this diverse universe of God and derived many valuable lessons therefrom. There are several objects in nature which teach valuable lessons imparting wisdom. The development of common sense consists in comprehending the origin and nature of such objects.

One should grasp the significance of history, culture and civilisation and propagate it. One who intends to undertake such propagation must first of all comprehend the nature of the soul. In this world there are several branches of learning like physics, music, literature, art and mathematics. Of all these forms of knowledge, self-knowledge is the sovereign. Without its attainment one cannot enjoy any peace. Though one may gain renown and recognition in the world, one will not experience happiness without Self-knowledge. "Knowledge of the Soul," "Knowledge of God" and "Spiritual Knowledge"—all these expressions connote that wisdom which promotes full awareness of soul and God. Self-knowledge is that knowledge by acquiring which everything else is known. A person with Self-knowledge can indeed be acclaimed as all-knowing.

Secular learning cannot confer on us abiding and absolute peace. Self-knowledge alone can help us cross the sea of sorrow. So all should strive to attain this Self-knowledge, which can be acquired through purity of mind. Purity of mind can be attained through pious deeds, sacred acts, charity, compassion and devotion. Disinterested action consecrated to God purifies the heart. The Sun of Wisdom dawns in a pure heart. The dawn of such wisdom exalts Man to the status of God.

Human effort constitutes the prime step in man's endeavour to attain this highest state of Godhood. God's grace is the second essential factor. Anyone can strive for and attain Self-knowledge. Men and women, rich and poor, all are eligible to kindle in themselves the flame of spiritual wisdom. Distinctions of race and religion, caste and creed do not come in the way. It does not matter if one has no secular education, no grounding in physical sciences, or is not well-versed in worldly lore. In the modern world it is not that easy to gain this Self-knowledge. All the same, one need not give up the effort in a mood of frustration and despair.

Some people relentlessly seek spiritual knowledge at the expense of secular learning. This is not desirable. They miss both and wander aimlessly between the two. Such a predicament too is undesirable. Secular learning should not be neglected. It is beneficial to acquire spiritual vision while seeking mastery over secular lore. So, youth should necessarily spend some time everyday in meditation upon God.

Young men have to spring into the sphere of action and strive to the best of their ability for the building up of a resurgent India, and a happy peaceful world. They must shed the desire for power. The desire to uproot corruption and immorality, and the urge to work hard should firmly be implanted in the heart of every student. Mother India's future depends on them and she is waiting for them. Even as it is the duty of children to serve and please their mother, it is the bounden duty of every child of Mother India to make her happy. To serve the Motherland selflessly should be the sacred ideal of one's life. Thus, it is the duty of all Indians to engage themselves in the dedicated service of Mother India. Such an obligation on our part may even be described as forming part of *"Desa niti"* (nobility of character of the individual vis-a-vis his motherland). Therefore, every student must inculcate in himself a wider perspective of national unity and integrity. A person without character can neither uplift himself nor be of any use to the country.

Sacrifice too is an aspect of character. It is one of the qualities which young men should imbibe. It is often thought that charitable and philanthropic acts make for sacrifice. But there is a vast difference between charity and sacrifice. Charitable people give only a fraction of their bounty to others. Gifts of land, distribution of food, contribution of physical labour and spreading of education and knowledge belong to this category. Through acts of charity no man ever gives up all that he has. One is not cursed to be born penurious if one does not perform acts of charity. Going a step higher some retain for themselves what is just and essential and give away the rest to society. Such people win the highest acclaim in the world. Our sacred texts prescribed that a portion of one's possessions must be offered to the poor and helpless. Neglecting this injunction, one should not accumulate *lakhs*[1] of rupees in a selfish, callous, unfair manner like an avaricious curmudgeon. Such a miser will become a victim of disaster and degradation, sooner or later. It is inevitable.

Wealth piled up through unfair means is the result of exploitation of the blood of the poor. Young men ought not to become slaves of such unfair existence and adopt exploitation as a means to living. Even God will not forgive such selfish, exploitative lives. He who piles up wealth

---

[1] Lakh - A lakh is one hundred thousand.

without enjoying or giving to others will be damned after death. The progeny of such people too will be damned.

There are four inheritors for hoarded wealth. The first is Charity; the second, the king. Fire is the third inheritor and robber, the fourth. The first claimant is Charity and the major share goes to him. Students should recognise the profound significance of this truth and utilise the wealth they acquire for the welfare of mankind.

Sacrifice is the highest step. One who has the true spirit of sacrifice gives to others without any hesitation or reservation, smilingly and gladly, even his dearest and highest possession. Surrendering the fruit of action to the Lord is real sacrifice. A *Tyagi* (One who sacrifices) does not shrink even to give up his body, regarding it as worthless straw. Sacrifice means something more than giving up of wealth, gold, and material objects. Evil qualities like hatred, jealousy, wrath and malice which have become ingrained in man over many lifetimes should be discarded. There is no happiness greater than that obtained from sacrifice. Only those who sacrifice are the children of immortality because they live forever.

When we study our epics and legends we come across numerous figures who embody such spirit of sacrifice. Emperors like Sibi and Bali , heroes like Dadhichi and Karna belong to that illustrious line. We need today such persons animated by the spirit of sacrifice among the political leaders and students. They should forget selfishness, crush egoism, dispel desire for power, and put an end to pettiness of mind, and pledge themselves to justice and to promote the welfare of society.

Unfortunately, words are losing their significance. Sacrifice, justice, righteousness, and service have lost their meaning and degenerated into business. Selfishness looms large and dances like a destructive demon among the students, politicians and educationists. Clamour for power and the desire for position are uppermost in the mind of man. Our country, which was once celebrated as a land of sacrifice, dedicated endeavour and penance, has degenerated into a veritable playground for ephemeral joys. And this is the reason for the country's many afflictions and ailments.

This state of things must come to an end and there should be a change for the better. Then our history will be repeated and our former glory revived. Thousands of sacrificing spirits should emerge from your midst. Every young Indian should be enriched once more by the spirit of sacrifice.

Sacrifice is sweeter than enjoyment. Sacrifice should become the aim of life. Only through sacrifice can one attain peace. Sorrows do not flee from us as long as the mind is not at peace with itself. Agonies dwell forever within us. Without the tranquillity of the soul, any amount of wealth cannot be of any use. Surrendering the fruits of action with a dispassionate mind is eligible to be termed sacrifice. Purity of mind alone can confer upon you tranquillity. The Upanishads have proclaimed in a full-throated voice that sacrifice alone leads to immortality. Sacrifice is the chief trait of the pure. Therefore, every student must imbibe and display the spirit of sacrifice in his life. He should not become a victim of the disease of enjoyment.

Unfortunately, there is a widespread opinion circulating freely that education is for jobs and not for the expansion of illumination. This is deplorable. Wisdom is illumination. It is the aim of education to radiate that light of wisdom. Such wisdom bestows upon man real power. Wisdom enables us to recognise mutual relationship of objects and individuals and to know the precedents and antecedents of each object.

How can this illumination enter man's being? By listening to and going through great books like the Vedas, the Vedantha, the Upanishads, the Koran, the Granth Saheb, the biographies of noble souls, books dealing with physical and technological sciences and psychology, one gains this light. Along with wisdom, discriminatory approach and logical thinking can be gained by reading them. One should not depend entirely on knowledge derived from sacred texts but depend upon wisdom arising from experience.

The shape and the content of education must change. Professor Gunnar Myrdal of Stockholm University visiting Delhi in 1972, said, "The educational system of India is not progressive. It fosters the mentality that we shall not soil our hands." All Indians, especially students, should recapitulate these words. This remark pinpoints the tendency of our students to lead comfortable lives under electric fans, resting in air-conditioned chambers, avoiding manual labour, its stress and strain, sweat and dirt, without even one fold of their ironed clothes getting crumpled.

This attitude is a far cry from the ideals of obedience and humility instilled by education. Students should impart to the people around them in society the sacred ideas they have imbibed. They must spring like tiger cubs into the arena of the villages and cleanse them of all sorts of pollution. They must teach and train the illiterate residents of the villages to live decently with dignity. Students must strive along with the villagers and lead them forward. Students of today should pose lofty ideals of life to the world through their exemplary lives.

✧ ✧ ✧ ✧ ✧

22. Eternal Truths

The Veda is the Mother of all the Sastras. The Veda emanated from God Himself as inhalation and exhalation. The great sages, who were the embodiment of the treasure gained by long ascetic practices, received Veda as a series of sounds and spread it over the world by word of mouth from preceptor to pupil. Since it was "heard" and preserved by generations, the Veda is known as Sruthi, "that which was heard or listened to." The Veda is endless. Who composed the Vedas? Until today, it has not been possible to unveil their names. Those who recited it had perhaps no desire to earn renown, for the names are nowhere seen mentioned in the Vedas. Maybe they had attached no importance to their names, or clans or sects, or it is likely they had no kith or kin or clan. Whoever he or they may be, the sages were sure they were masters of all knowledge, for the sense of equality and equanimity found in the Veda is the innate quality of only such wise persons.

So it is very appropriate to infer that the Veda was given to the world only by persons endowed with all powers.

The word "Veda" originated from the root "*Vid*," meaning "to know," "*Vidam thu anena ithi Vedah.*" "That which reveals and makes clear all knowledge is Veda." The Veda can be mastered neither by limited intellect nor by limited experience. The sacred Veda instructs all that one requires for his spiritual advancement. It instructs one in the means and methods to overcome all sorrows and grief. It instructs one in all the spiritual disciplines which can give unshaken peace. No one has understood correctly the beginning of the Veda or its end. So, it is hailed as *Anaadi* (Beginningless) and Sanathana (Eternal). Since the first and the last of the Veda are not known, it is Nitya, Everlasting. The intelligence of humans is tainted but since the Veda has no trace of taint, it is concluded that it cannot be a human product. So the Veda is also characterised as *Apourusheya* (Non-personal).

The Veda is its own authority. Each Vedic sound is sacred because it is part of the Veda. Those who have faith in the Veda and its authority can personally experience this. The great sages were enriched by such experiences and they have extolled it as the source of wisdom. These experiences are not bound by time or space. Their validity and value can be recognised not only in India but by people of all lands. They lay down basic truths, it can be asserted.

The Vedic religion originated, we do not know when; others came later. This is the difference. So, if the Absolute has to be known, it is not possible to succeed with the help of the skill and strength that man has. Human intelligence can operate only within certain limits. *Buddhigrahyam atheendriyam* (The intellect transcends the senses). But the Veda is beyond the reach of intelligence. Intelligence is restricted. It can deal only with facts discoverable by the senses and experiences related to these. It can act only in the area of the visible, the viable.

Mother Veda has been kind to her children—the human race. To sanctify its cravings and to uplift the race, she has posited the concept of Time—and its components, the years, months, days, hours, minutes and seconds. Even gods were declared to be bound by Time. The individual or Jiva is caught in the wheel of Time and Space and rotates with it, unaware of any means of escape. But really he is beyond the reach of Time and Space. The Veda is bent upon the task of making him know this Truth, and liberating him from this narrowness. Mother Veda is compassionate. She longs to liberate her children from doubt and discontent. She has no desire to inflame or confuse. Wise men know this well.

Gravitation has existed on earth since we do not know when. It had its origin along with the Creation of the Earth. The Earth and the Force of Gravitation are both inseparable, indistinguishable. Just because it is not recognised by a few or because it is not visible as such, it will be foolish to deny its existence in the earth. But the fact is, no one knew the existence of this universal force, though it was there along with the Earth! The force was operating even when man was unaware of it. At last, after analysing various principles and observing various experiments, the Western physicist, Newton, announced that the Earth had the force of gravitation. The world accepted his statement and placed faith in its truth. But the force was operating all the time, even before the announcement by Newton. It did not start operating all of a sudden, when the experiments demonstrated it.

The Vedas are Eternal Truths. They existed even before the people of this land discovered, practised and experienced them. Just as Western physicists announced the existence of gravitation after their experiments, the ancients of this land demonstrated the innate authenticity of the Vedas through their own experience. Here too, the Veda existed long before it was discovered and put into practice. Newton's Laws of Gravitation benefited the whole world. They express universal truths applicable to all places and times. They are not confined to Western countries only. So too, the Veda is Truth, not merely for Bharath but for all people on earth.

It is not correct to claim that Bharath, or India, is the birthplace of the Vedas. The utmost that can be said is that they were discovered by the people of Bharath. To ask why a happening in one place did not take place in another place also is the sign of a confused mind. The Divine Author decides what should happen when and where. As He decides, so it takes place. The atmosphere in India was congenial for the revelation and the growth of the Vedas. The Vedas were drawn towards the hearts of the sages of this land, this *Karma bhoomi* (earth), this *Yoga bhoomi* (land of Yoga) and this *Tyaga bhoomi*. Other lands pursued *Bhoga* (luxury) and so their atmosphere was overcharged with worldly aspirations and achievements. The Vedic message could not therefore be easily understood there. Since in India, the spiritual quest was sincerely pursued, along with material objectives, people here had the good fortune of the *Veda Matha*, Mother Veda, incarnating.

Of course, this does not mean that the Veda Matha has not blessed other lands or is absent therein. It is like the force of gravitation, present everywhere. The Veda is omnipresent. The heroic sages of Bharath were able to receive the Vedic Message as a result of their sadhana of denial and detachment as well as their capacity to concentrate and to experience the bliss resulting from practising it. They were so selfless and full of compassion and love that they shared with those who approached them what they had heard and enjoyed. They are therefore called "*Manthra Drishta*." Through the long line of their disciples, the message has come down the ages and spread all over the land. Like a continuing flood, the mysterious Veda was "visualised" by the Sages as Drishtas. The Bharathiyas, people of this country, are well aware of this debt.

The scriptural texts of India—the Vedas, Vedangas, Upanishads, Smrithis, Puranas and Ithihasas—are repositories of profound wisdom. Each of them is an ocean of sweet sustaining milk. Each is sacred and sanctifying. The waters of the Ocean can never be diminished in volume however many pumps you ply to drain them. Enormous quantities of water are turned into steam by the hot rays of the sun, bundled into clouds, and returned to the earth as rain. This helps the harvesting of grain and renders the land green with vegetation. The wonder is that in spite of this tremendous uptake and downpour, the level of the ocean does not go down even by an inch. Furthermore, even though thousands of live rivers pour their waters into the seas, the level is not seen to increase. Similarly, the persons who have supplemented their knowledge of the scriptural texts with the awareness of their validity acquired by practising the lessons contained in them, are not affected by praise or blame, whatever the source and quantity. Their hearts will stay pure, unaffected and calm. The holy scriptures of India are strongholds of such sustaining lessons.

However, one can imbibe those lessons only to the extent of one's patience and intelligent skill. After mastering the texts and gaining experience in putting the lessons into actual practice, one can share the light and the joy with others. The texts of India insist on the value of actual practice and the need to confirm the truths by experiencing their impact.

If a person desires to understand clearly the sacred books and scriptural texts of India, to imbibe their message, he must learn the Sanskrit language. He cannot avoid that responsibility and that duty. The very mention of Sanskrit immediately arouses in many among us a prejudicial attitude. "It is the dead language of a dying culture. It is boosted by the fanatic attachment of antiquated conservatives," contemporary moderns declaim. They condemn the language as surviving only in meaningless formulae, in fast-vanishing rituals and ceremonies, in wedding rites and other futile exercises. It is a very difficult language to learn, it is said. Such beliefs have dug themselves deep into the minds of moderns. These banal opinions and false attitudes have to be exorcised from the minds of men.

Sanskrit is an immortal language. Its voice is eternal. Its call is through the centuries. It has imbedded in it the basic sustenance from all the languages of the world. Revere Sanskrit as the Mother of languages. Do not ignore its greatness or talk disparagingly about it. When you yearn to slake the thirst for nectar offered by the Vedas, you have to learn Sanskrit. In order to interpret the Vedas and elaborate their inner meanings and mysteries, the sages have left behind text books of complementary sciences like grammar, poetics, philosophy and astrology. Their researches and books range over several fields of knowledge like astronomy, geography, jurisprudence, ethics, epistemology, music, psychology and rhetoric. Western scientists are struck with admiration at the wonder of astronomy they have unveiled and the truths they have unravelled in other sciences. They have benefited by the clues provided by these sages, and they are engaged in further research encouraged by the discoveries of these ancient seers. They have acknowledged that these Rishis had advanced far more than the Greeks in their astronomical knowledge. In the Vedas and the supplementary literature they produced, we can find already revealed many secrets of nature, hailed as revolutionary discoveries by modern science, like the existence and explosive possibilities of the atom. Many sections of the *Atharvana Veda* are found to be mines of such important information when examined by westerners. The Germans established special institutes and universities in order to conduct research on the contents of the tons of palmleaf manuscripts of the Naadi texts and horoscopes, and on astronomy, medicine, chemistry, toxicology, mathematics, etc. They are learning Sanskrit so that this work may proceed successfully. In America, Russia and even in Afghanistan, the Universities are not only themselves eager to introduce Sanskrit as a subject of study but they are being pressed by scholars to do so! Foreigners are revering these texts from India as gems of lucky discovery.

The science of Yoga was assigned great prominence in the past by Indians. Even now, in many countries of the world this science is being studied and practised. Institutions where *yogasanas* are taught exist in great numbers throughout America and Russia. In India, however, when the practice of Yoga or Meditation is mentioned, people respond with the feeling that it is a spiritual path related to the Vedantic school of thought. As soon as Yoga is referred to, many who hear the word get pictures before their minds of lone hermits in the depths of thick forests, wearing the ochre robe of monks and living on fruits, tubers and roots. Their opinion is that Yoga-sadhana is the ancient discipline practised by such homeless ascetics. This is an ignorant guess. It is not true at all. The Yoga science is today being probed by physicists and others in Western countries.

In this era of technology, it is becoming increasingly difficult to lead peaceful lives. Men are becoming the targets of various types of mental ailments. In countries on the front line of civilisation like America and England, people have lost the delight of natural sleep at night. They experience only artificial sleep induced by the tablets they swallow. As a consequence of these and many other drugs taken to ward off other ills, they suffer more and more from diseases of the heart and blood pressure. In the end, they render themselves unhealthy wrecks. Such lives are highly artificial. People are sunk in fear and anxiety; mentally on one side and physically on the other. They have no rest. Drugs, tablets, capsules and pills are produced in millions but the general health has not improved. Besides, new varieties of illness have emerged and are developing fast. A few intelligent westerners have realised that their only refuge is Yoga. They have confirmed their conclusion by means of experiments. They have taken to Yoga with increasing faith.

The Vedas are the oldest literary creations of man. Now the word "literature" is used to connote writings scribbled while eager to find something to spend the time hanging on hand. They have no inner worth or significance. They destroy the traits of good character in the reader and implant bad attitudes and habits. They do not adhere to the path of Truth. But literature is a term that cannot be applied to writings or poems that reel off tales that are false. It should not emerge from the egotistic fancies of the individual.

The Vedas are the soul that sustains the spiritual life of Bharath. They are the breath that keeps the people alive. They possess a divine power, amazing in its effects. They are charged with the vibrations of manthras, which can be experienced by those who go through the process scientifically. They can impart also the strength derivable through symbols and formulae of Tantric nature. "Tantra" means the means and methods of utilising the manthras for one's own good. Man has physical and material power only. His Karma becomes holy and sacred when the mechanics (*yantra*) of life are ruled by Manthra and Tantra. The technique of this sadhana is in the Karma Kanda of the Vedas. The ancient sages became aware of this and have preserved it for mankind in the Four Vedas.

Unable to grasp these truths, those who pride themselves as "moderns" proclaim that the Vedas contain only verses and manthras which are learnt by rote and repeated by aged cronies. Not only "moderns" but even those who earned distinction as "the foremost Pundits," those who expound to the people, gathering fame, use the

Vedas for promoting their material well-being and not for helping them on the spiritual path. They are unable to discover the sacred task for which the Vedas exist. Whenever the chance arises, they benefit by the scholarship, but they are not eager or able to use the Vedas to purify their daily lives.

As a result, "moderns" find it impossible to develop faith in the Vedas. When the Pundits do not seek to Practise the Vedas they have learned and parade their lack of faith by not instructing their own children on the glory of the Vedas, they naturally cause lack of faith in the entire society.

Many others, in spite of their ignorance of the meaning of the Vedic hymns, walk through busy places reciting the sacred texts in mechanical orthodoxy. Foreigners—especially German scholars—though they have not learnt the Vedas by rote, have realised that the manthras possess and transmit profound power. They have during the centuries carried to their own country, portions of the Vedas and conducted patient and painstaking research on them. Consequently, they have unravelled strange mysteries. They found that the Vedas contain the secrets of all the arts which confer progress on man.

As adjuncts to the Vedas, many scriptural texts emerged. The Veda (knowledge) of Archery, and Veda of Ayu or Maintenance, Prolongation and Preservation of Life (medicine), the Veda of Planets and Stars (Jyotir Veda)—many such texts were composed and promulgated.

Sage Viswamitra discovered the manthra named Gayatri, which is addressed to the energy of the Sun, Surya. This manthra has infinite potentiality. It is a vibrant formula. It has immense powers, powers that are truly amazing. For, the Sun is its presiding deity.. The Gayatri enabled Viswamitra to use rare weapons which bowed to his will when the manthra was repeated with faith. Through the powers he attained in this way, Viswamitra was able to become a great scientist and create a counterpart of this cosmos. A person who is able to increase the capabilities of his hands and his senses is now considered a "scientist." But the term (*Vijnani*) was correctly applied in the past only to those who developed spiritual power and discovered the formulae for delving into the Divine within, those imbued with faith and devotion who could spontaneously demonstrate that power in actual day to day living. On the other hand, the "scientists" of today know only a bit here and a bit there. They exaggerate and boast of what they have managed to learn. They are fond of pomp and proud display. They rise sky-high on the fumes of praise. Such absurdities are quite contrary to the true behaviour of a scientist. For he is humble and meek. He is aware that, however much he knows, there is a far vaster field which he has yet to know. He is conscious that Divine Grace is responsible for what little he knows.

Viswamitra was a scientist who had recognised this truth. So, there is no scientist yet greater than he was. But though a sage of such immense eminence and with so expansive a heart lived in India, he is not remembered by the people of this land. They honour the foreigners who have glimpsed his greatness. They have placed their faith in those researchers who have elicited valuable lessons from the Vedas. The Veda is the Mother of Bharath. But the children do not revere the mother any more. They revere the stepmother and believe in her! This is the result of the anglicised educational system.

Probing further and further into the scientific attainments of the sages of ancient India, the construction of *Vimanas,* vehicles capable of flying in space, is described by Sage Bharadwaja. Mental Science had advanced so much that they could reproduce what had happened or predict what would happen. The Science of Medicine was highly developed in India. It was Sage Bharadwaja who taught this science for the benefit of mankind. Sage Atreya took up the task of propagating this science and technique of healing. Saint Charaka compiled all the discoveries into a *Samhitha* or "Collection," named after him. It deals elaborately with the diagnosis of diseases, methods of healing and cure, foetal development and other essential but not easily discoverable facts of medical science. The doctors proficient in that science could, in those ancient years, surgically remove or correct various diseased parts of the body when the illness could not be cured by drugs. Saint Susruta has written in his compendium on many surgical processes. This text has been discovered and is available for study. Dhanvanthari, Nagarjuna and other sages have brought to light many other medical discoveries of Ancient India, made by adherents of the Vedic tradition of scientific research. There are also many valuable texts on ethics, jurisprudence and other social sciences which are invaluable treasures for all time, like the Dharma Sastra of Manu and the Nyaya Sastra of Gautama.

Vedantha is the legitimate property of every section, every caste, every community, and every race, of the followers of any faith and persons of both sexes. Vedantha means Wisdom or Jnana. "Wisdom" relating to which field of knowledge? It is wisdom on the knowledge of the Atma. This wisdom is the supreme gain that can be earned in life. What greater gain can there be for man than becoming aware of his Self, himself knowing himself. Faith in the possibility of knowing oneself is necessary for every student of Sruthi (the Vedas) and Smrithi (the Moral Codes).

The object seen is clearly separate from the subject who sees. This is a universally accepted Truth. Who is this I that sees? All things that have Form are recognised and seen by the sense organ, the eye. The eye sees the physical body, other individuals, even insects, worms and things. It sees everything that is within its range. The body too is a *thing* that the eye sees, along with the rest. So, how can we conclude that the body *is* the I?

Then, who really is this I? Fire burns and also brightens. It burns things by heat and brightens them by the light it sheds. Fire is different from the things it acts upon. Now, who is it that knows this truth—the truth that "fire" and the "things that it burns" are different? It is the Atma. When a log burns, the fire is present and active in *all* of it. Similarly, the Atma pervades the entire body, and enables it to perform deeds and to move itself and its limbs.

The light shed by the lamp is the instrument that informs us at night: "This is the cup." "This is the plate." The eye is a similar instrument which informs us "This is a house," "This is a thorn," "This is a stone." The eye is not the Atma. In the absence of the lamp, the eye, or in the absence of the eye, the lamp cannot cognise the house, the thorn, the stone, the cup or the plate. Both the lamp and the eye are media or instruments of "illumination."

The instrument, eye, sees the body, where it is situated. The body that is *seen* cannot therefore be other than a similar instrument. The senses are the experiencers of hearing, tasting, seeing, touching and smelling. When the eye is known as an instrument, the other four senses too have to be recognised as tools. All these senses are under the control of the mind which is their master. Even this mind is being controlled and conditioned by some other master. The mind cannot be the core of man.

The intellect or buddhi examines the information materials offered by the mind. It is the instrument that judges and decides. For example, imagine a sharp knife. However sharp, it cannot cut a fruit on its own initiative. Nor can it cut the thinnest thread by itself. It can do so only when it is held by the hand of someone. The intellect is similar to the knife. It is helpless without the "I," the Atma, which has to wield it.

Then, we have to consider another equipment of man—the Prana or the vital air. Let us consider whether we can nominate it as the "I"? During deep sleep, man is not conscious that he is breathing and that the "vital airs" are alert! Of the three states—the waking (*Jagrat*), the dreaming (*Swapna*) and the sleeping (*Sushupti*), though the prana is existent in all, the man is not aware of the experiences of the waking state while dreaming, nor of the experiences of the dreaming state while in the wakeful state. During sleep, the pranas do not activate the intellect or the memory. They appear to be quiescent. When the boss is active, the dependants cannot keep quiet. Since they are not uniformly active always, pranas or the Prana principle cannot be considered as the "I" or Atma.

Now about the Ego. There are two fields in which it operates and so, it has two meanings: (1) Self love, *Ahamkara*, the "*Dehatma,*" Body-consciousness, the Exterior "I" and (2) the Inner "I," the *Pratyag-Atma*. Persons who do not know this distinction confuse themselves and assert that "I" is applicable to the Dehatma. But this is wrong. The body as we have seen is a tool, it is an object. It is the seen and not the seer. How can the ego, identified with it, be the Atma? This ego also is of the "seen" category. It is absent in sleep and plays false in dreams. Truth has to persist unaffected, in the past, present and future. That which is absent in two states, how can it be true?

As a result of this inquiry, it has become plain that the senses, the mind, the intellect, the vital airs—not one of these can be accepted as Atma and accorded that validity. Therefore, the question arises: what else, who else, is Atma?

It has no entry or exit, no hands and feet, no organs and limbs, no blot or blemish. It is the minutest among the minute, the hugest among the huge. Like space, it is everywhere. It *is* all and so it is free from "I" and "mine." It is consciousness, as fire is heat, and the sun is light—it has no affinity with distress or delusion. It is supreme everlasting ecstasy, *Paramananda*. It is the core, the heart of all beings. It is the awareness in all. It is the seer of everything "seen," it sees all objects seen. Everyone, whatever his nature or stature, who declares, after being served by the senses, "I see," "I hear," "I taste," etc., is really only talking of lamps, of tools and not of the Atma. The Atma is not a part-seer, a series-seer, a non-seer or a pseudo-seer.

The Buddhi, like the moon, has no light in itself. Like the moon it reflects light from another source adjacent to it, namely the Atma. Buddhi can operate only by reflecting the Cosmic intelligence, represented by the Atma.

The Sun is designated the Cosmic Eye, Jagat Chakshu, a name based on the Sun's involvement with the proximity to other objects. The Sun has no ego-sense or a sense of possession and property, and no will or want or wish. By His very presence darkness disappears and light envelopes the world. So, He is called the Enlightener. But He is not consciously doing so, as if in duty bound. The Atma too has neither obligation nor application. If asked how the Atma becomes a "doer," the reply is—is the magnet a "doer," simply because the needle which is in its neighbourhood moves?

The basic question may now be raised. Does the Atma exist? If it does, how and with what proof can it be established? There is no need to prove that the Atma exists, for, if the Atma is capable of being proved by certain arguments and lines of reasoning, the existence of a person, who uses those arguments and follows those lines of reasoning has to be posited. That person will again be the Atma!

Of course, some men may reply that the Vedas are the authority for the existence of the Atma and that the Atma can be experienced and validated through the Vedas. The Vedas do prohibit certain activities as Unatmic or opposed to the norms expected from a believer in the Atma. They do recommend certain other activities like charity, moral behaviour, as Atmic. But the Atma is its own proof, its own witness. Its existence cannot be established by other facts, or things.

The Sastras, which are texts supplementary to the Vedas, declare that God resides wherever six excellences are evident: Enthusiasm (*utsaha*) determination (*sahasam*) courage (*dhairya*) good sense (*sadbuddhi*) strength (*sakti*) and adventure (*parakrama*). The inaugural prayer of man has to be directed to God (Ganapathi) to gain these six gifts which can purify consciousness and reveal the Atma. One has to undertake the discovery of one's Atmic core, with bravery in the heart. This is no exercise for cowards. Wicked persons, waverers in faith, doubting hearts, woeful countenances, are destined to go through life as *rogis* (sick persons) and not yogis (dwellers in Atma).

This is the distinguishing mark that separates the wise (jnani) from the unwise (ajnani). Krishna spoke, laughing with an outburst of joy. Arjuna listened while overpowered by sorrow. The jnani is always full of joy, he laughs. The ajnani is afflicted with sorrow, he weeps.

In order to achieve victory while inquiring into the nature of the Atma, one has to pass through the *Asramas*—the four stages of life recognised and recommended by the scriptural texts of Sanathana Dharma. Each one while passing through each stage, aware of the duties and responsibilities prescribed in the texts, learns for himself a quantum of the knowledge that leads to Atmic awareness.

It is only after the childhood years that the Asram routine will have an impact on man. Until then, he cannot gather any special knowledge about his duties and responsibilities. Man has boyhood, adolescence, youth, middle age and senescence, as stages of growth. There are also corresponding stages in the growth of wisdom in him.

In the first stage of boyhood, he is led from ignorance and "innocence" into the world of knowledge, when he is accepted as a pupil by a Guru (Preceptor). After that, he has to serve the Guru and obey him, without feeling burdened and bound. In the second stage of youth, he has to share with society the means and measures for its progress and security. He has to start earning for his livelihood and spending his income with intelligent care. He has also the duty of providing examples to those younger than himself and guide them into socially useful paths. At the same time, he must follow the footsteps of elders and learn from them lessons for his own advancement.

In the third stage of adulthood, intelligent attention has to be paid not only to one's own advancement and the advancement of the family and society but also to the advancement of the people generally. That too is the responsibility of the grownups and they must acquire the skills necessary. They must have wider visions of the peace and prosperity of all mankind, and try to contribute to both, within the limits of their capacity and resources.

Old age is the fourth stage. By the time one reaches this stage of his journey, he must have discovered that the joys available in this world are trivial and fleeting. He must be equipped with the higher knowledge of spiritual joy, available through delving into the inner spring of bliss. Through his experiences, his heart must have softened and be filled with compassion. He has to be engrossed in promoting the progress of all beings without distinction. And he must be eager to share with others the knowledge he has accumulated and the benefit of his experiences.

Thus, occupations and resultant attitudes have been assigned to the various stages of human life. Practice is as important for confirming one in wisdom as reading is important for confirming one in knowledge. Alongside of knowledge, youth has to cultivate the good qualities of humility, reverence, devotion to God and steadfast faith. He has to engage himself in good works and enjoy them for the sheer elation they confer. During adulthood, along with the earning of wealth and involvement in the improvement of society, attention must be paid to the promotion and preservation of virtues and to the observance of moral codes. Steps should be taken for improving one's righteous behaviour and spiritual sadhana. All levels of consciousness have to be purified and then directed to holy tasks.

During middle age, besides fostering the family and society, man has to live an exemplary life to inspire his children and hold forth, before society, elevating ideals worth practising. No attempt should be made to belittle society and benefit only the family, for, it is bound to fail. The Brahmam principle can be realised only by purifying one's activity and utilising that activity to serve oneself in all. It can never be realised so long as one relies on the caste into which he is born, or the intellectual equipment he has added unto himself or the mastery of the Vedas.

He who is born cannot escape death, sometime, somewhere. Every moment, many are born and many die. But man has to discover how to "avoid" death. Now, the Atma which is the core of man, is not born. Since it does not take birth, it does not meet death. Death happens to the body with which it is associated, with which it mixes. The delusion that the body is the core, that the body is real, *that* verily is death. Affliction by that falsehood is the act of dying. To be free from that delusion is to attain Immortality. The body it is that disintegrates, not the Atma, the Soul, the Self. The body is undergoing change every moment and the final change is death, when the Self, changeless, remains. When one believes that the changing body is oneself and starts referring to it as "I," that "I" dies, but the real "I" is deathless.

As intense elevating activity and fearless inquiry into one's Truth are practised more and more, the consciousness that the "body is oneself" can be overcome and negated. Consider the fruit of the tamarind tree. When unripe, it is not easy to separate the rind, the pulp and the seed. So too, those who have stuck to sensual desires and to fondling and feeding the body, cannot earn the awareness of the Atma. When the tamarind fruit becomes ripe, the rind can be broken off, the pulp gets detached from the seed and the seed can be isolated without effort. Inquiry and unselfish activity ripen the consciousness and the Atma can be isolated from the body, clear and pure.

The body has five encasements which hide the Atma. These are grouped under three categories—the gross, the subtle and the causal. The physical case (flesh, blood, bone, etc.) and the vital case (breath) form the gross body. When these two sheaths, the *sthoola* body (the gross body), fall or disintegrate, the body too falls and cannot rise.

The word *sukshma* which is generally translated as "subtle" means in Sanskrit "small"; it has another meaning too, "that which expands." Air expands more than water. Space is more expansive than air. Compared with the expanse of the liberated soul, even space has to be considered "gross"! Steam is more expansive (subtle) than water. Though a block of ice or a lump of camphor appear "gross," they become subtle when heated or lit.

The rule of the world is that the seen causes the unseen, the manifested explains the unmanifested. But the rule in the realm of the Spirit is different. The latent Atma causes the patent world. Being is behind Becoming, and finally, Becoming merges in Being. The patent is absorbed into the latent. As milk from the cow, from the Supreme Person flows the Power of Maya or Relativity as the Five-element constituted Cosmos (Prakriti), the patent manifestation. The Cosmos is cognised as a composite, just as milk is a composite of cream, curd, and butter, which can be got out of it by the action of heat and cold, and the addition of sour drops, and the process of churning thereafter. The churning separates the butter from the milk. In the same manner, through cosmic processes and upheavals of heat and cold, the Five Fundamental Elements, (earth, water, fire, air, and space) were separated and Earth, this Ball of Butter, emerged, as the product of the churning. If any person or thing has one of the three character traits (balanced, passionate, dull) predominant in the makeup, we denote him as having that trait. So also the Element, which is predominant in any created entity, gives its name to it. This is the reason why the world on which we live is called Bhoomi, the Earth. The realms in space where the element of water predominates are known as *Bhuvar Loka* (Subtle world) and *Swar Loka* (Causal world). The materials therein flow in currents and streams.

In short, what appears as the Five Element-constituted Cosmos is only the superimposition on God, of the non-real Individual Self and the Five Elements. God seen in and through the non-real appears as Nature. This is but a distorted picture of reality, this ever-changing multiplicity. The fault is in the mirror that reflects, the mind that perceives, the brain that infers. What the mirror presents as true has no authenticity. The mirror is coated with dust and its face is not plain at all. God has no maya. He has no intention or need to delude, nor does He will that it should happen. But man in his ignorance sees things which do not exist and believes that they do exist just as he sees them. This weakness of his is named *Adhyasa*.

When God is reflected as Nature, the reflection becomes Maya. As milk curdles into yoghurt, God becomes

Jagath or the World of incessant transformation, or Maya, or the Image of the Unchanging Divine. His Will causes this unreal multiplicity on the One that He is. He can by His will end it. He is the Master of Maya.

God is omnipresent, omnipotent. Of the three entities, the Overself, the Self and Nature, Nature has, as its purpose, the fulfilment of the wants of man. God has no wants or wishes. He is the fullest and highest Attainment. The Ananda *of* every Being and *for* every Being flows spontaneously from God. His words to Arjuna in the Gita are, "I have no duty to discharge, Oh Partha, in the three worlds." He has created duties only to foster the consciousness of all living beings. He has no activity and no obligation. He brings about the result for every activity. Without Him, no activity can yield result! He decides which result should accrue from which act.

✧ ✧ ✧ ✧ ✧

23. Modes Of Worship

The Veda is the most ancient as well as the most lasting knowledge (or Sastra) discovered by man. That is to say, man has not invented it. He has only recollected it in the serene silence of the soul. So, the Veda can lead man into the Vision of the Truth, unreachable by the senses and unrelated to the material world. It is inaccessible to human reason because it is transcendent. So, it is described as *Paramam Vyoma*, the Great Protector, also Indestructible, Thath, Truth. These words denote all the four Vedas, beginning with the Rig Veda.

The term Veda was originally applied to the Supreme Lord, Parameswara, the All-knowing. *Veththi ithi Vedah*—(He who knows is Veda). Then it was applied to the principle of understanding *Vedayathi ithi Veda*, (that which makes known is Veda). The Rig and other Vedas have the all-knowing characteristic. So this meaning too is appropriate.

Later the word was applied to activities in consonance with the Vedas—activities promoting the goals laid down, namely, Righteous, Economic, Volitional and Spiritual.

The Supreme Lord is All-seeing. He is the Person on whom all the hymns of the Vedas converge. The Vedas enable man to get the vision of that Lord and those who have earned that Vision are the Rishis. They were guided by the Vedas. Many psalms, hymns and declarations emerged from them. As a result, the Supreme Lord Himself is referred to as the Great Sage (Maharshi) in the *Brahma Sutra*. Among the 108 Names of Shiva, the Supreme Lord, we find *Maharishi* and *Mukhyarishi* (the Chief Sage, the Foremost Sage). Even the Veda is personified and referred to as Rishi, for the same reason. Brahmam (the Vast Expanse) is another word which denotes the Supreme Lord as well as the Veda. Hence, all acts, undertaken with no other desire than the attainment of Brahmam, are also known as Brahma activity—a Brahma Yajna. A Rishi Yajna is a sacrificial act—with no desire to earn the fruit ensuing therefrom—designed to gain the Vision of Truth.

While performing such sacrificial acts and Yajnas, the expression, *Swaaha*, is used. Yajnas are pure, auspicious, sacred acts. This exclamation Swaaha, used while offering oblations or reciting the Veda, is full of significance, *Kesavaaya Swaaha* (Offer it to Lord Keshava [Krishna]), *Praanaaya Swaaha* (Offer it to the vital airs), *Indraaya Swaaha* (It is offered to Indra): the expression is used in this manner. The meaning generally given is "Let this be duly consumed. May these materials we are now placing in this holy fire be fully accepted and consumed, so that through this Fire they can reach the Deity for which it is intended—Kesava, Prana, Indra." Doubts may arise—why pray to Fire for something which is inevitable, because it is the very nature of Fire to burn all that is put into it. But the scriptural meaning is different. Kalidasa in the poem "Kumara Sambhavam" describes the Himalayas as *Deva-thaatma* (Divine Souled), that is to say, the Embodiment of the Divine. The scriptures distinguish the Divine Body and the Material Body, which each entity and being possesses. The Divine Body of everyone cannot be cognised by the senses. When an oblation is given to it, it becomes sanctified. The *Aahuthi* (oblation) is transubstantiated into *Havis* (A special offering of food during Vedic ceremonies).

The oblation or Aahuthi is thus described in the Veda. The offering and offeree become one through the acceptance. (The *Attha* (offerer) and the *Adya* (Offeree). Who in this case is the offeree, and acceptor? It is Agni, the Divine Power inherent in Fire, in the Sun, in the Warmth of the Vital Air that sustains Life. When with the recitation of the appropriate ceremonial formulae, material oblations are placed in Agni with the phrase Swaaha, it is not a mere exclamation. It is expiation; it is realisation of the prayer, which the ritual represents.

The Veda is known as Chhandas also. This name means pleasant, joyous. It is also associated with the kindred meanings—strong, vital, shielded. Since all the attributes and characteristics can be predicated of the Vedas, the name referred to above is very appropriate. The sacred ceremonies and rituals which the Vedas expound confer joy not only on the participants but on the entire world and even on worlds beyond. The Supreme Lord who is the source of Bliss, is known in the scriptural texts as *Yajnaanga* (having the Vedic ritual as His Limbs), *Yajna-vahana* (using the Vedic ritual as His Vehicle). When Godhead assumes Form the first manifestation is *Hiranyagarbha* (the Golden Womb). This too is embodied Bliss, having as vehicle the Bird with wings of Beauty, or Garuda. The Supreme Lord is also known as *Vrsha-ratha*, He whose chariot is the Bull, the symbol of Dharma (Righteousness). This is the reason why in temples we find the bird Garuda carved or kept as an idol before the shrine of Vishnu and the figure of the Bull or its idol placed before shrines of Shiva.

Chha or Chhaadana has as its root meaning another important aspect of the Vedas—shielding, fostering or promoting, promoting the welfare, the ultimate liberation of humans engaged in the unceasing round of worldly affairs. Humans are ever caught up in activities pursued with the profit available as the purpose. They have to be moulded as righteous men and women at the same time. The Tree of Life has to be guarded to offer them fruits and shade. The Veda has to shield from destruction the activist "doers" (Karma lovers) from the evil temptation to court unrighteousness, and the inquiry-fond thinkers (Jnana seekers) from the evil temptation to pursue the pleasure-bound senses. Since the Veda both guides and shields, these verses are called, in totality, Chhandas. Through their role as armour or shield, they shower Bliss on all who rely on them. "*Chhaadanaath chhandaasi.*" By shielding they become "chhandas."

There is a myth about the Vedic rituals, collectively known as Yajna. Once, Yajna fled from the gods taking the form of a black antelope. The gods went in pursuit, but they succeeded only in retrieving its skin. That skin became the Yajna, the symbol of the rite. The white, dark and tawny colours on that skin represent the Vedas, Rig, Yajur and Sama, and it was adored as sacred for this very reason. It was honoured as symbolising the Triple Knowledge, that is to say, Mastery of the three Vedas. The skin is used by the officiating priests and other participants in all Vedic ceremonials in order to invoke the protecting hymns, called Chhandas. The three colours are believed to represent the three worlds too, and therefore, he who is seated on the skin or wears it benefits the three worlds by his Vedic recitations and oblations.

The master of the ceremonials at the Vedic Yajna is described in the Vedic scripture as the "Foetus in the Womb." As the foetus is safe and secure, with its fingers clasped and body prostrate enveloped in the mother, the priest-initiate must be enveloped in the antelope skin symbolising Mother Veda. To human eyes, it is just a skin but during Vedic rites, it becomes a shield. This is the reason why, before wearing it, the initiate prays, addressing it, "You are the shield, Charma, shield me as Charma." Charma since it shields man from grief, injury, and wrong has come to mean happiness and bliss. Vishnu, the second of the Trinity, is the embodiment of Bliss. And Vedic sacrifices confer bliss. Vishnu is praised as Yajna itself (*Yajno vai Vishnuh*). The Lord Vishnu is the embodiment of the Triple Veda.

Upasana means the acquisition of the Presence of the Divine, the achievement of the Bliss of adoration. Vedic tradition sanctions four paths as legitimate and fruitful to win this achievement. They are called *Sathyavathi, Angavathi, Anyavathi* and *Nidaanavathi*. We shall consider these in some detail.

Sathyavathi: The scripture defines the Divine thus: "*Sarva Vyaapinam Aatmaanam, Ksheere sarpith iva arpitham*"—The Atma is immanent everywhere, just as ghee interpenetrates every drop of milk. When the seeker pursues the Truth with this conviction urging his endeavour, his sadhana is called *Sathyavathi* (Truth-based). "*Maaya thitham idam sarvam, jagada-vyaktha moorthinaa,*" the Lord declares. "In My latent form, I am in entire Creation, operating the mystery. See in Me all this, see all this as Me." When one succeeds in this effort the Sathyavathi path will lead to success. "I shall be visible to you as all this and in all this," the Lord assures. The Lord promises this Vision of Immanence and Transcendence to whomsoever that persists with sincerity on this Sathyavathi path.

Angavathi: The Universal being is the Fire, the Wind, the Sun, the Moon and all else. He is the Breath that sustains life in all beings. He is the Fire that illumines all. He is the Rain that feeds the plants that provide sustenance. So, He can be adored either as Fire (Agni) or as Wind (Vayu) or as Rain (Varuna), as having graciously assumed all those beneficent forms. This approach through the benign manifestations of Angas, is the Angavathi path. Anga means a "limb," a "fact," a "feature."

Anyavathi: Picturing the many-faceted Divine and symbolising, in perceivable ways, the attributes that are evidenced in each facet, the seeker endeavours to acquire the Presence of the Divine. One form of the Divine, the Omnipresent Vishnu is pictured as having the Conch (symbol of the Primeval word or Sound), the Wheel (symbol of Time) and the Mace (symbol of Might and Majesty). With the facet to which is ascribed the power and willingness to overcome obstacles (*Vighneswara*), the single tusk symbolising sharpness and concentration is associated. Easwara or Shiva (the facet of disintegration and dissolution) has the *Soola* or Trident (symbolising in its three prongs, the Past, the Present and the Future). Rama, the form of righteousness or Dharma is always pictured with the *Kodanda,* the bow which can send the arrow (will) straight to the target. Krishna, the manifestation of Universal love, has on His Crown a peacock feather, symbolising the thousand-eyed glance of Grace. He bears a flute on which He plays enthralling tunes. The flute is the symbol of the egoless, desireless seeker. The facet of Wisdom pictured as the Goddess Saraswathi, has a Veena in Her hand. The Veena is a stringed musical instrument, symbolic of heartstrings responding, with harmony and melody, to the gentle touch of the True, the Good and the Beautiful. Seekers meditate on these pleasing Personifications and the significance of the symbols of their attributes and adore the Divine in the delight that wells up in their hearts. This is named the Anyavathi Path—the path through symbolised Divinity. *Anya* meaning the other, the adjunctory, the appurtenance.

Nidaanavathi: This path is slow but progress is always achieved when each step is successfully negotiated. *Sravanam* (listening to the Glory of God), *Kirtanam* (singing joyously His unique graciousness), *Vishnoh smaranam* (keeping in memory and recapitulating always the Majesty and Mercy of the Lord), *Paada sevanam* (aspiring to fall at the Feet of the Lord), *Archanam* (offering prayers to the image or idol of the Lord), *Vandanam* (offering gratitude for blessings received), *Dasyam* (surrendering to the Will of the Lord), *Sakhyam* (confiding completely in Him), *Atma Nivedanam* (dedicating thought, word and deed to Him), *Thanmaya aasakthi* (longing to merge in Him) and *Paramaviraha-aasakthi* (agony at the slightest separation from Him)—these are the eleven stages which the seeker has to pass through to win the final consummation in Bliss. Hence, the name for this path is "slow and sure" (*Nidaana*).

These four paths (Sathyavathi, Angavathi, Anyavathi and Nidaanavathi) are each one progressively more commendable than the previous ones, as far as simplicity and practicability are concerned. They award, in the end, Oneness with the Universal Will. Of the various other Upasanas or sadhanas which are mentioned in the sacred texts and practised by seekers, *Pratheekopasana* (Idol Adoration) or *Prathiroopopasana* (Image Adoration) is included under Angavathi Upasana "*Sarvathah paani paadam thath, sarvathokshi Siro mukham*"—(Everywhere His Hands and Feet, everywhere Head and Face). The Lord (Madhava) has His Hands everywhere, for He is in all. He sees through all the eyes. He thinks, plans and resolves in all heads. He eats through all mouths, hears through every ear. Through one Form, you can adore Him as all Forms. This is the highest ideal—He is latent in all beings. He operates unseen in and through all. This is the Prathiroopa-upasana, worshipping Him as present in each. There are sundry other Upasanas (steady worship) too mentioned in the texts:

Bhanopasana: Ascribing to the Lord the highest splendour, the deepest compassion, the most potent power, etc. and worshipping Him as such.

Geethopasana: Adoring Him as the Master and Preceptor who teaches the Gita and reveals the Way. The epic *Mahabharatha* is revered as a Veda, the fifth one. It sets out the code of morality that man must adhere to for realising his goal, both here and hereafter. It is an inexhaustible treasure chest of guidelines for righteous living and spiritual uplift. Here, the Lord can be seen on the theatrical stage of *Dharmakshetra* (Field of Dharma), with all the equipments and roles, the plots and counter-plots, the denouements and devices, for the Cosmic Play He is enacting in His own marvellous way. That play is the epic, the *Mahabharatha.* In this play, the actors and actresses, the dialogues and texts, the cues and songs, have been assembled by Him. He is the cast, the director, the audience—all. It is Madhava who manifests Himself and manipulates in every thing and being. On one side, boundless material strength urged on by unrighteous greed, and on the other, the apparently limited strength of the Atman, the ever-righteous. In the Cosmic Confrontation and conflict between these two forces, the Lord stands forth as the arbiter, the supreme embodiment of the victory of Right over Might. This is the ultimate ambrosia available in the *Mahabharatha*—the *Bhagavad Gita*, the Song of Divine Triumph. The core lesson which the epic is bent on teaching is contained in the Gita—the seeker surrendering, with the words, "*Karishye vachanam thava*" (Your word shall be obeyed) and the Lord admonishing the seeker, "*Swadharme nidhanam sreyah*" (In fulfilling the duty assigned to you lies your safety and prosperity.) All work should be tested on this criterion.

The path of dedication to the Will of God (Bhakthi) should not be discarded, for it can lead you to all-round delight and bliss. Instead, if one closes his eyes and instils into himself the conceit that He is Brahmam, he will miss the joy and become a victim of anxiety. When you pound husk you cannot expect rice grains to result, can you? And Krishna is no other than the very Brahmam!

Adwaithopasana: "The body of the cow has milk in it. The milk has ghee in it. But the ghee cannot be a source of strength to one. The milk has to be drawn, yeast added to curdle it, butter has to be churned out and clarified to produce the ghee which, when consumed by one can give one strength. So too, though God is omnipresent and omnimotivating, He has to be discovered and cognised in order to realise Bliss, Awareness. Like oil in mustard, butter in yoghurt, like water inside the earth, like fire in timber, God is present but not patent in everything. God is in the human body and in the human mind. To become aware of Him there, spiritual effort is necessary. When that is undertaken, the unity of both can be realised. One will not thereafter experience "two" or "difference." The awareness of the one without a second is "Liberation," release from bondage.

Visishtadwaitha: (qualified Monism) Ramanuja considered the problem whether the God whom one seeks to worship and realise as real must be conceived as being apart from oneself, or whether God can be conceived as in oneself. His answer is: Life is the soul of the body. God is the soul of Life. God is the grantor, the force, the sustainer.

Seek Him in that spirit. The Supreme Sovereign Purusha in whom all the elements reside and who is the indweller and inner motivator of all Creation, can be known and experienced only by winning Grace through surrender. Understand well His transcendence and immanence, and realising one's deficiencies, surrender the ego in order to partake of His Glory. The mental attitude of the seeker should be "*Thwam eva sarvam, mama deva deva.*" (Thou alone art all, Oh my God of Gods. You are the urge, you are the path, you are the goal.) The spiritual effort must be one-pointed, unwavering, untiring.

Dwaithopasana: (Dualism) The dualistic outlook on the relationship between God and the individual is that of husband and wife. Vishnu, the Lord, the ever-free ever-full, has to be adored as the wife adores the husband. Among such sadhakas, Chaithanya is most noteworthy. He established a distinct *Chaithanyopasana* itself. Without the anguished yearning for the Feet of Lord Krishna liberation cannot be gained. Why? Even purification of one's intelligence is not possible without that yearning. This is the assertion of Chaithanya. He declares that sages and others capable of being immersed in inner bliss can enjoy the ecstasy of the supreme consciousness through the contemplation of the auspicious, restorative and cleansing attributes of the Lord, Sri Hari. No text or scripture is needed for one to realise this bliss. Sunk in the waves of that Divine ecstasy, the person ignores all the norms of social behaviour and escapes from all conventions. He sings aloud the names of

Hari, sheds streams of joy, dances in divine delight and experiences unadulterated genuine bliss. He feels that the Lord's Feet have made every inch of ground holy. Thus they sing the glory of the Lord fully attuned to Him. This sadhana was emphasised, as the easiest and most fruitful, by Chaithanya. His foremost goal was to attain the absence of body consciousness in the flood of ecstasy that surges from melodious group-singing of the majesty and mercy of the Lord.

There are a few other forms of worship which merit mention. The *Gowdeyopaasana* is one such. Sri Krishna, formulated and incorporated in the unmanifest Immanence, as Purushotthama and Radha, formulated and incorporated as unmanifest Universal Energy, are both visualised, and known as Krishna-Radha or more commonly, Radha-Krishna. Madhava is another name of Krishna, signifying that He is the master of Cosmos or Prakriti. So, the name used in this Upasana or worship is Radha-Madhava. The recitation of this Name is held by the adherents of this path of worship to be capable of leading to the ecstasy that can confer liberation from all forms of bondage. The *acharyas* or founders of this Upasana declare this to be the attainable goal. The Lord is the very embodiment of the nectar of delight. Living beings can get immersed in spiritual delight only when they imbibe that nectar. The Sruthi texts proclaim that those born in Ananda can live only in and through Ananda. The sacred name Radha-Madhava is the key, it is said, to the treasure-house of that precious nectar.

Radha-Madhava is Prakriti-Purusha and this dual category is assumed to represent the duality of Jivatma and Paramatma, the Individual Soul and the Universal Soul, the Wave and the Ocean. Worship is offered to both through that Name. Vallabhacharya proclaimed "*Krishnasthu Bhagawan Swayam*" (Krishna is the Lord Himself). Attaining Him was explained to be equal to merging in the Universal, the goal of genuine monists.

Saivopaasana is also a notable path. This emphasises the worship of Shiva as formulated in the Lingam or Symbol. "*Lingam Sarva Kaalam.*" The Infinite Lingam is the symbol of the primal energy which forms the basic cause of the origin, condition and progress of the "elements" that compose the Cosmos. The Lingam is the Form of Shiva Himself and realising it as such is asserted as the ultimate goal, liberation.

Virasaivopaasana advocates the worship of Shiva, the Lord or Easwara, as the one and only, everywhere and always. The merging of the individual in the splendour of the Linga or Easwara is the acme of all sadhana, the achievement of Liberation.

Paasupathopaasana: The individual entity (Jiva) is tied by the bond (*paasa*) of the qualities or modalities arising from nature. Pasupathi (Shiva) is worshipped in order to earn freedom from bondage.

Saakthopaasana: "*Sarva Deva mayee Devee*" (Devee is all Gods). The Primeval Universal Energy, *Aadi*

Paraa Sakthi, is conceived as the matrix of all forms of Divinity. The Cosmic Urge, the Prakriti, is the cause of the variety and multiplicity of expression, the manifold forms. The Maheswara (Supreme Divinity) has this capacity to manifest and is therefore so named. Maheswara and Parasakthi are two aspects of the same force. This dual-faceted force motivates the Universe, from the vast expanse of the sky to the entire earth. The unmanifest Supreme Person manifests as the Feminine Universal, the Maya, the Paraa Sakthi. In each individual, it is experienced as knowledge, strength and activity.

Jainopaasana: (The Marwari [money lenders]) community, in worshipping the Lord, adopt a Vaishnavite slant. Idols of Vishnu, with the traditional equipment of the conch, the wheel, the mace and the lotus, are found in Jain temples). The Jains have as their manthra:

Namo arihanthaanaam
Namo Siddhanaam
Namo ayiriyaanaam
Namo uvajjhayaanaam
Namo Loye sabba saahoonaam,

meaning:

Salutations to the great heroes (Mahavira) who have conquered desire, etc.

Salutations to the Siddhas (those equipped with super natural powers)

Salutations to the great Masters of Spiritual Wisdom

Salutations to the great Teachers who transmit the wisdom

Salutations to the good persons of all lands.

This fivefold adoration helps remove the evil effects of all sinful acts. Experiencing the meaning of this manthra gives one the sum of prosperity. The Jains declare that when one merges in this universal adoration, one is liberated and attains Moksha.

Sikh-upasana: The Preceptor (Guru) who reveals the Atma and makes one conscious of Its existence as one's reality, has the highest place in this system of worship. The collection of the teachings of the Gurus—referred to as *Granth Saheb*—is extolled and revered by the Sikhs. It is derived from the spring of Bharathiya spiritual traditions. Its ideas form the very core of Bharathiya cultural traits.

Christ Upasana: Lord Jesus is the Saviour. Man is by nature prone to fall into sin, knowingly or unknowingly. Jesus shed his heart-blood on the Cross to free man from sin and cleanse his soul. Follow this Lord and his teachings contained in the Bible and worship him—this is Christ Upasana. Sing his glory and adore him through hymns—this is the mode of worship which this Upasana envisages.

Muhammadan-Upasana: "*Imaamdaaree khaidaa mey ho, Pygambar mey bharosa.*" Acquire self-confidence and place all burdens on God. Have implicit faith in the Power of God every moment of living, recognise it at every step—these are the rules for meaningful life. One has to evidence one's rectitude in the *Durbar* (palace) of the Lord, when one lays down his body. So, one has to follow the straight path laid down by the Lord until the very end. For this, the Holy Koran is the guide. It has to be revered and observed down to the very letter. This is the spiritual instruction to be observed in this Upasana.

"*Allaho Akbar; La Illah Ill Allah.*" This is the sacred formula of Islam. It signifies that God is the supermost sovereign, Allah is the undisputed unexcelled Ruler of Creation. He alone is worthy of worship. In the *Bhagavad Gita*, Lord Krishna says, "There is nothing higher than Me." The Koran formula says the same. The Muhammadan Upasana too is a Form of the same spiritual practice, based on the same Truth.

All these Upasanas reveal that, since man initiated his age-long inquiry into his own truth, he has accumulated, especially in Bharath, a vast spiritual treasure which can save him from sorrow and bondage. The treasure is so vast and so deep that it has survived the passage of centuries as vast and as deep as ever it was, unaffected by the emergence of different modes or the influx of other forms of worship.

Besides, the spiritual wisdom of India is today a triumphant beacon, shining in One resplendent flame in the thickening darkness, illumining all lands, encompassing all races and enchanting all mankind.

There is no fortune more splendid than being born on this sacred land, Bharath, repository of this magnificent and beneficent culture, which can save the world. Becoming aware of this blessing is, indeed, a spring of immeasurable Ananda.

✧ ✧ ✧ ✧ ✧

24. The Divine Body

The sociological basis of Bharathiya culture has to be clearly understood. Mankind falls into four groups, when innate nature and inclination are considered. They are named Brahmin, Kshatriya, Vaisya and Sudra. This demarcation is not a selfish, crooked conspiracy designed to make the "superior" trample upon the "inferior." Nor is it the consequence of an envious plot to obstruct human progress. It is best to judge it as a plan to promote the expansion of human achievement by fostering the trends and traits of each person. It is the royal road for the attainment of human progress. It works only for the promotion and regulation of human activity in such a manner that harmony and social well-being are ensured.

The Gitacharya, Lord Krishna, has declared, as readers already know, "*Chaathurvarnyam mayaa srishtam guna karma Vibhaagasah tasya karthaa-ramapi maam Viddhi akarthaaram avyayam.*"

"I have created the four Varnas, the Brahmin, the Kshatriya, the Vaisya and the Sudra, on the bases of natural disposition and vocation of each. Know Me to be author of these, as also the non-author, the Unchangeable."

The system of caste is thus founded on attributes and activities. The world was in the very beginning predominantly Sathwic in nature and as a consequence all were only Brahmins. Later, through the adoption of various vocations and the development of various inclinations and preferences, types of people got demarcated as castes. The one and only Brahmin class of Rishis and Sages had later to be sectionalised, in the interest of social justice and harmony, when qualities of character varied. In the Santhi Parva (*Mahabharatha*), Sage Bhrgu has elaborately answered a question raised about this development by Sage Bharadwaja. It runs as follows: "Brahmins fond of worldly pleasures affected by egoism, subject to anger, lust and other passions have Rajo Guna mixed with their innate Sathwic nature, and so they are classified as Kshatriyas. In fact, all Brahmins cannot be predominantly Sathwic in nature, nor can all of them be devoted to pure ritual activity. Those who do not adhere to the Sathwic ideal of Truth and who evince the qualities of Thamo Guna mixed with Rajasic traits, those who are mostly both Thamasic and Rajasic were classed as Vaisyas. The rest, who spend their lives in occupations involving violence, who do not practise cleanliness and who are bogged down in Thamasic means of livelihood were classed as Sudras. Thus, the Brahmins denoted various castes and ensured the safety and security of human society. This is the assertion of the scriptures, the Sruthis."

Those endowed with pure Sathwic characteristics are Brahmins. Those with Rajasic qualities, and as a result, equipped with courage and heroism are Kshatriyas who can protect mankind from harm. Those who have neither valour nor heroism but who are proficient in persuasive talent and the tactics of commerce and eager to use these skills in proper methods are Vaisyas. In this class, Rajo Guna and Thamo Guna are blended. The others who have no inclination for undergoing asceticism or acquiring scholarship, who do not practise sadhana, who have no physical stamina and mental courage necessary for battle, who do not possess the special skill needed for trade and commerce, are Thamasic in nature and so engage themselves in Thamasic professions. These are the Sudras. They fulfil themselves by their labour through which they contribute to world's prosperity and peace.

The above four castes are only limbs of one body, they are not separate entities. There is no basis to consider that one is superior and another, inferior. Each performs its function so that the body can be healthy and happy, so that each can win the highest state of consciousness from its own role. So the ancient Vedic Varna organisation based on such broad ideals was taken to be the divine Plan. The Plan witnessed the truth that the four castes were the four limbs of the one Divine Cosmic Person or Purusha.

This truth becomes clear when we consider the Divine statement in Purusha Sukta found in the Rig Veda.

Braahmanasya mukham aaseet
Baahoo raajanyoh Krithah
Ooroo thad asya yad Vaisyah
Padbhyaam Soodro ajaayatha.

In this declaration, those with pure Sathwic nature and established in higher knowledge or wisdom, that is to say, the Brahmins, are declared as the face of the Cosmic Person; those who are predominantly courageous, physically strong, having in their nature Sathwic and Rajasic qualities, the Kshatriyas, as the arms of the Cosmic Person; those who have Rajasic nature mixed with Thamas and are efficient in the arts of commerce, the Vaisyas, as the thighs of the Cosmic Person; those who are active and engaged in physical labour, those endowed with Thamas, the Sudras, as the feet of the Cosmic Person. The Lord is thus described in the *Rig Veda* as the wondrous and splendourous embodiment of such components.

But this holy and profoundly significant Varna organisation fell into the hands of unintelligent selfish men with restricted outlook and narrow ideals. They expounded it in writing as their fancy dictated. Thereby they brought about great harm to the world. As a result, the system is interpreted today as a plan designed by the majority to suppress the minority!

Caste is the Cosmic Person Himself manifesting as Human Society. It is the visible form of the Lord, charming in every limb. It is a great pity that this truth is not widely recognised. It is the good fortune of this land, Bharath, that in this Vision, the Lord, as the physical integration of the "caste limbs" is promoting peace and harmony, prosperity and well-being for all mankind. Not aware of this truth, people declare that this system is only a manmade contrivance and that in fact, all men are equal. They base this conclusion on external characteristics and breed agitations on the basis that all mankind is one species. Of course, it is true all men are of one species. But distinct groups do emerge as a result of differences in character and the professions they adopt. This is an inevitable development. No one can deny this. All are not Sathwic in this world of humanity. Only very few are of this nature. Judging from mere appearance, one cannot declare that all men are one. We have to distinguish and discriminate and group those with Sathwic, Rajasic, Thamasic, or combinations of one or more of those natures, separately. No one can say this is wrong.

In a general way, predominantly Thamasic natures are grouped as Sudras. But among them, have we not many who are of pure Sathwic quality? Among those who are grouped as Brahmins, the pure Sathwic type, have we not many who are predominantly Thamasic? Therefore, the Vedic Religion of Bharath has clearly laid down that appearance alone, or birth in a family alone cannot decide caste. It has to be determined on the basis of character and occupation.

The four Varnas are the limbs of the Divine body, of the One and Only Lord. Each is important and indispensable for its own role. The goal of each is to serve the Lord by service to man, rendering it in accordance with its Dharma, the accredited mores of conduct and modes of behaviour.

Some people assert that the Sudras have neither the right nor the responsibility to practise spiritual sadhana or tapas and that the Brahmins have it. What we have to remember here is that the restriction is for the Sudra nature, not for individuals born as Sudra; the permission is for the Brahmin nature, not for all individuals born as Brahmins. Cows are useless as animals for riding. Horses are useless as yielders of milk. These statements are based, not on hatred of the species or malice against any of them but on the nature and characteristics of the animals concerned. Both are quadrupeds. However, their distinct natures decide that one is useful for the milk it yields and the other, for riding purposes. The castes are not based on race or birth but on innate nature and tendencies, and profession adopted and pursued.

All sparks are fire. There is only one Caste, Humanity. They cannot be declared separate nor is there any need to assert that they are not separate. So too, men or individualised beings are not separate from Brahmam or the Universal Absolute. Nor is there any need to assert that they are not separate. The relation between Brahmam and Jiva is not one of identity or oneness, but it is one of cause-effect.

Until liberation is attained, the particular is distinct, is separate. When liberated, since the cause of individualisation is absent, the Jiva is one with Brahmam. Separation and oneness of Jiva and Brahmam are the consequences of the delusion of bondage and the awareness of freedom.

Brahmam is self-effulgent, self-illuminating. It is not the "object" of consciousness. It cognises all objects. All things and beings belong to the category of "seen" or "observed" or "known." It is the seer, not the seen. When the form is the "seen," the mind is the "seer." When the mind and the activities of the intellect are the "seen" or "observed," then the witnessing Consciousness is the seer.

This Witness can be seen by no one. All things cognisable are the body of the Atma, not the Atma. They are name-form combinations like pots and pans of clay which impinge on the consciousness as "seen" or delude it like the "silver" on "mother-of-pearl." The Atma is; It exists by and for Itself. The Universe is the "other," for others; it is "real" and available for others. The Universe has no innate Reality. It emanates from Brahmam and its reality is based on the reality of Brahmam. So, its reality is lower than that of Brahmam.

The illusion created by a magician for deluding others cannot affect the magician himself. In the same manner, since the Universe is contrived by Brahmam, it is clear that it cannot affect Brahmam itself.

The Universe or Jagath appears to have emanated, as being experienced as such and as disintegrating. These three are but superimposed ideations upon the One modificationless Reality, just as the snake superimposed upon the rope at dusk. This ideation is Maya, for it hides and reveals at the same time. Maya cannot be said to be unreal. The rope appearing as snake is known again as rope, when the snake disappears. But the Universe does not disappear in the same manner. Its existence cannot be explained away. It is a phenomenon that is unique. We cannot compare it with any other. We cannot dismiss it as unreal or accept it as real. It is Sath-asath, not asath. That is to say, Real-unreal, not unreal.

It persists for some time and is therefore real. It does not persist for all time and is therefore unreal. A thing can be true only as long as it is not something different. While dealing with it on the temporary, practical, relative level, the Universe remains as Universe. It is relatively real. Truth is One, it has one feature only. The Universe has manifold features through Time, Space and Causation. So, it is unreal. Sankara proclaimed the Jagath or the Universe to be unreal. When the highest Truth is known, the Universe is revealed as but an appearance on the Real and as distinct from the basic Brahmam. Since the Jagath is imposed by the mind on the Brahmic Truth, it too is to be treated as a Brahmic phenomenon. "*Sarvam Khalvidam Brahmam*" (All this is indeed Brahmam).

In fact, Brahmam and Maya have an intimate relationship. Truth, once established and fixed, is ever unaffected. And Maya is not fundamentally true. That which is learnt by the impact of appearance is pseudo-knowledge, Mithya jnana; it is Avidya (non-knowledge). The Mithya (delusion) or Avidya will vanish as soon as the Appearance is negated and the Truth is grasped. Maya is neither invalid nor valid. The Universe appears to each in accordance with the point of view or the angle of vision. It has no independent existence, apart from the ideations that are projected by and from the observer. Its support and sustenance is Brahmam. Brahmam is the unaffected Cause. The effect will not have any effect on it. Maya is the effect that is prone to inevitable change. Brahmam is the One Supreme Truth, which has assumed the manifoldness of the Jagath (Cosmos), consequent on the influence of Maya. When Brahmam is cognised as with Maya, it becomes the material Cause of Jagath. It is in the Jagath as Jagath. Brahmam is said to be the instrumental Cause of the Jagath but Maya is the prompting influence. Brahmam is beyond both cause and effect. It cannot be a cause, either instrumental or material.

The Jagath can be conceived as a picture, of which the plain canvas is Brahmam and the colours spread on is Jagath, the appearance immanent on the canvas. The human figures are dark. The Jiva is the experiencer of pain and grief through his involvement with the Jagath. He is the "seen," "the observed." Brahmam is Truth; Jagath is the

Play, the Pantomime, the Sport. It is the manifestation of the Will that is latent in Brahmam. To recognise the Will behind the Play is the attainment of liberation.

Dhyana (Meditation), *Puja* (Worship), Karma (Rites and Rituals) and other activities are laid down for those too dull to recognise this Will. Only those who can renounce the fruits of worldly endeavour can claim the right to follow the path of Wisdom (Jnana). Sadhakas on the Vedantic path must be equipped with (1) the discrimination to distinguish the transient from the eternal, (2) determination to desist from worldly and other-worldly pleasures, (3) acquisition of sense control, self-control, detachment, fortitude, faith and equanimity and (4) keen yearning for liberation.

All things have to be viewed as the products of the Divine Will and used with the reverence that this knowledge will kindle in the Consciousness.

The path of holy activity and the path of intellectual discrimination, of Karma and Jnana, are intended for different Sadhakas. It is not possible to mix the two and follow them together. Righteous living can confer new life. Prosperity is the gift of the knowledge of Dharma. Liberation is the gift of the knowledge of Brahmam. The awareness of Brahmam does not demand, for its continuance and constancy, the practice of any sadhana. It does not depend on the performance of any specific duties and chores.

Liberation is of two kinds: Immediate and Gradual. The first is the result of the attainment of wisdom, Jnana. The second is the result of Upasana, spiritual study and sadhana. Jnana is pure unmixed monistic experience. Bhakthi or Devotion is of the nature of Supreme Love, characterised by the Love for God, for the sake of the Lord only.

✧ ✧ ✧ ✧ ✧

SRI SATHYA SAI BOOKS AND PUBLICATIONS TRUST
PRASANTHI NILAYAM

PIN 515 134, ANANTAPUR DISTRICT, ANDHRA PRADESH, INDIA
IMPORTER / EXPORTER CODE NO. 0990001032
RESERVE BANK OF INDIA EXPORTER CODE NO. HS-2001198

THE VAHINI SERIES : (BOOKS WRITTEN BY BHAGAWAN SRI SATHYA SAI BABA)

	Price Rs.	Wt. in Gms. approx.
Bhagavatha Vahini (The story of the Glory of the Lord)	44.00	490
Dharma Vahini (Stream of Righteousness)	22.00	230
Dhyana Vahini (Stream of Meditation)	20.00	210
Geetha Vahini (The Divine Gospel)	32.00	415
Jnana Vahini (The Stream of Eternal Wisdom)	15.00	165
Leela Kaivalya Vahini (The Cosmic Play of God)	9.00	75
Prasanthi Vahini (The Supreme Bliss of Divine)	15.00	140
Prasnottara Vahini (Answers to Spiritual Questions)	15.00	95
Prema Vahini (The Stream of Divine Love)	20.00	125
Rama Katha Rasa Vahini Part-I (The Sweet Story of Rama's Glory)	48.00	705
Rama Katha Rasa Vahini Part-II (The Sweet Story of Rama's Glory)	37.00	460
Sandeha Nivarini (Clearance of Spiritual Doubts)	18.00	230
Sathya Sai Vahini (Spiritual Message of Sri Sathya Sai)	30.00	406
Sutra Vahini (Stream of Aphorisms on Brahman)	19.00	110
Upanishad Vahini (Essence of Vedic Knowledge)	18.00	225
Vidya Vahini (Flow of Spiritual Education)	17.00	210

SATHYA SAI SPEAKS SERIES:
(DISCOURSES BY BHAGAWAN SRI SATHYA SAI BABA) (REVISED & ENLARGED EDITIONS)

	Price Rs.	Wt. in Gms. approx.
Sathya Sai Speaks Vol. 1 (Years 1953 to 1960)	34.00	390
Sathya Sai Speaks Vol. 2 (Years 1961 to 1962)	39.00	490
Sathya Sai Speaks Vol. 3 (Year 1963)	38.00	420
Sathya Sai Speaks Vol. 4 (Year 1964)	39.00	510
Sathya Sai Speaks Vol. 5 (Year 1965)	43.00	535
Sathya Sai Speaks Vol. 6 (Year 1966)	59.00	465
Sathya Sai Speaks Vol. 7 (Year 1967)	40.00	410
Sathya Sai Speaks Vol. 8 (Year 1968)	39.00	425
Sathya Sai Speaks Vol. 9 (Year 1969)	30.00	345
Sathya Sai Speaks Vol. 10 (Year 1970)	35.00	450
Sathya Sai Speaks Vol. 11 (Years 1971 to 1972)	45.00	565
Sathya Sai Speaks Vol. 12 (Years 1973 to 1974)	42.00	535
Sathya Sai Speaks Vol. 13 (Years 1975 to 1977)	30.00	445
Sathya Sai Speaks Vol. 14 (Years 1978 to 1979) (Part 1)	30.00	270
Sathya Sai Speaks Vol. 14 (Years 1979 to 1980) (Part 2)	34.00	490
Sathya Sai Speaks Vol. 15 (Years 1981 to 1982)	40.00	550
Sathya Sai Speaks Vol.16 (Year 1983)	30.00	330
Sathya Sai Speaks Vol. 17 (Year 1984)	32.00	325
Sathya Sai Speaks Vol. 18 (Year 1985)	25.00	365
Sathya Sai Speaks Vol. 19 (Year 1986)	30.00	405
Sathya Sai Speaks Vol. 20 (Year 1987)	39.00	460
Sathya Sai Speaks Vol. 21 (Year 1988)	35.00	455
Sathya Sai Speaks Vol. 22 (Year 1989)	35.00	475
Sathya Sai Speaks Vol. 23 (Year 1990)	44.00	510
Sathya Sai Speaks Vol. 24 (Year 1991)	40.00	540
Sathya Sai Speaks Vol. 25 (Year 1992)	40.00	645
Sathya Sai Speaks Vol. 26 (Year 1993)	50.00	655
Sathya Sai Speaks Vol. 27 (Year 1994)	35.00	510
Sathya Sai Speaks Vol. 28 (Year 1995)	43.00	620
Sathya Sai Speaks Vol. 29 (Year 1996)	43.00	635
Sathya Sai Speaks Vol. 30 (Year 1997)	35.00	490
Sathya Sai Speaks Vol. 31 (Year 1998)	53.00	730
Sathya Sai Speaks Vol. 32 (Year 1999) - Part 1	27.00	370
Sathya Sai Speaks Vol. 32 (Year 1999) - Part 2	27.00	370
Sathya Sai Speaks Vol. 33 (Year 2000)	39.00	495
Sathya Sai Speaks Vol. 34 (Year 2001)	38.00	462
Sathya Sai Speaks Vol.35 (Year 2002)	40.00	525
Sathya Sai Speaks Vol.36 (Year 2003) - Part - 1	29.00	330
Sathya Sai Speaks Vol.36 (Year 2003) - Part - 2	23.00	250

	Price Rs.	Wt. in Gms. approx.
Sathya Sai Speaks Vol.37 (Year 2004)	38.00	400
Sathya Sai Speaks Vol.38 (Year 2005)	29.00	325

SATHYAM SIVAM SUNDARAM SERIES:
(Life Story of Bhagavan Sri Sathya Sai Baba)

Sathyam Sivam Sundaram Vol. 1 (Birth to 1961)	60.00	595
Sathyam Sivam Sundaram Vol. 2 (1962 to 1968)	49.00	515
Sathyam Sivam Sundaram Vol. 3 (1969 to 1972)	48.00	425
Sathyam Sivam Sundaram Vol. 4 (1973 to 1979)	40.00	430
Sathyam Sivam Sundaram Vol. 5 (1980 to 1985)	55.00	605
Sathyam Sivam Sundaram Vol. 1 to 5 (Deluxe Edition)	390.00	350

SUMMER SHOWER SERIES :
(Discourses on Indian Culture and Spirituality by Bhagavan Sri Sathya Sai Baba)

Summer Showers in Brindavan 1972	15.50	230
Summer Showers in Brindavan 1973 (New Enlarged Edition)	46.00	789
Summer Showers in Brindavan 1974 Part - I (New Enlarged Edition)	36.00	360
Summer Showers in Brindavan 1974 Part - II (New Enlarged Edition)	38.00	380
Summer Roses on the Blue Mountains (Ooty) 1976 (New Enlarged Edition)	34.00	360
Summer Showers in Brindavan 1977	17.50	175
Summer Showers in Brindavan 1978	46.00	510
Summer Showers in Brindavan 1979 (New Enlarged Edition)	34.00	325
Summer Showers in Brindavan 1990	25.00	275
Summer Showers in Brindavan 1991	22.00	285
Summer Showers in Brindavan 1993	23.00	200
Summer Showers in Brindavan 1995	34.00	280
Summer Showers in Brindavan 1996	19.00	205
Summer Showers in Brindavan 2000	34.00	460
Summer Showers in Brindavan 2002	25.00	300

CHILDREN'S BOOKS:

Chinna Katha-Part I	30.00	350
Chinna Katha-Part II	42.00	385
Chinna Katha Illustrated	17.00	80
Chinna Katha Picture Stories Vol - 1	25.00	205
Chinna Katha Picture Stories Vol - 2	25.00	205
Chinna Katha Picture Stories Vol - 3	25.00	205
Chinna Katha Picture Stories Vol - 4	25.00	205
My Life is My Message	17.00	115
Stories for Children : Part I	17.00	190
Stories for Children : Part II	28.00	325
Divine Stories Vol 1 (Human Value Stories)	36.00	430
Divine Stories Vol 2 (Human Value Stories)	30.00	375
Ramakatha Rasavahini Pictorial - Vol. 1 - Purnima Ray	27.00	115
Ramakatha Rasavahini Pictorial - Vol. 2 - Purnima Ray	31.00	145
Ramakatha Rasavahini Pictorial - Vol. 3 - Purnima Ray	32.00	155

OUR OTHER PUBLICATIONS:

Baba - The Breath of Sai by Grace J. Mc Martin	46.00	485
Bhagavan Uvacha Series Vol - 1	75.00	540
Bhagavan Uvacha Series Vol - 2	75.00	450
Bhagavan Uvacha Series Vol - 3	85.00	–
Bhagavad Gita (Part - I and II)	69.00	820
Birthday Blessings of Bhagavan	25.00	325
Be Like Jesus	30.00	320
Grama Seva is Rama Seva	20.00	255
Conversation with Bhagavan Sri Sathya Sai Baba by Dr. John S. Hislop	29.00	375
Fundamentals of Sri Sathya Sai Educare Vol. I - Compiled by Ranvir Singh	60.00	520
Fundamentals of Sri Sathya Sai Educare Vol. II - Compiled by Ranvir Singh	59.00	510
Fundamentals of Sri Sathya Sai Educare Vol. III - Compiled by Ranvir Singh	59.00	625
Fundamentals of Sri Sathya Sai Educare Vol. IV - Compiled by Ranvir Singh	64.00	625
Finding God by Charles Penn	50.00	705
Food for Thought	40.00	465
Gems of Wisdom	53.00	690
Guidelines to Active workers of S.S.S.S. Organisations from Bhagawan Baba	19.00	195
His story as told by Himself	29.00	300
Ati Rudra Maha Yajna – August 2006 (with divine discourses and talks by eminent scholars)	30.00	330

A Recapitulation of Baba's Divine Teachings by Grace J. Mc Martin	35.00	485
A pioneering attempt at child labour elimination - A tribute to Sai Baba, The Ultimate Motivator	35.00	335
Seva: A Flower At His Lotus Feet - Grace J. Mc Martin	29.00	325
Spirituality and Health by Dr. (Mrs) Charanjit Ghooi	60.00	725
Bhakthi and Health by Dr. (Mrs) Charanjit Ghooi	30.00	270
Benedictory Addresses (21 Convocation Discourses by Bhagavan as Chancellor from beginning up to 2002)	26.00	350
Easwaramma The Chosen Mother (Enlarged edition)	24.00	285
End of the Endless Search by P.P. Arya	28.00	265
Sathya Sai Education in Human Values	25.00	280
Garland of 108 Precious Gems (108 Holy Names of Bhagavan)	15.00	170
Journey to God - Part II - J. Jagadeesan	86.00	645
Loving God - N. Kasturi	52.00	725
Love of Conscience - Rita Bruce	29.00	305
Life is a Game Play It - Joy Thomas	42.00	465
Life is a Challenge Meet It - Joy Thomas	26.00	330
Life is Love Enjoy It - Joy Thomas	28.00	345
Life is a Dream Realise It - Joy Thomas	32.00	335
My Baba and I - Dr. John S. Hislop	42.00	455
My Beloved - Charles Penn	35.00	395
Nama Mahima	16.00	160
Namasmarana	8.00	55
Ocean of Love	500.00	1865
One Single Stream of Love	41.00	210
Pathway to Peace Prasanthi	21.00	235
Purifying the Heart - John Goldthwait, Ph.D	20.00	215
A Practice for Purifying the Heart - John Goldthwait, Ph.D	8.00	75
Rays of Radiance - Service Adoration Illumination - Prof. K. Anil Kumar	37.00	440
Sai Sandesh - Prof. K. Anil Kumar	43.00	275
Universal and Practical Teachings of Bhagavan - Prof. K. Anil Kumar	24.00	305
Sai-Chology - Prof. K. Anil Kumar	45.00	460
Sadhana - The Inward Path	41.00	475
Sai Baba - The Ultimate Experience - Phyllis Krystal	35.00	435
Sai Baba - The Holy Man and Psychiatrist - Dr. Samuel H. Sandweiss	58.00	440
Spirit and the Mind - Dr. Samuel H. Sandweiss	46.00	545
Sai Bhajanamala	45.00	570
Sai Baba's Mahavakya on Leadership (Hard Bound) - Lieut Gen. (Retd) Dr. M.L. Chibber	52.00	460
Sai Advent - Compiled by Harendra Singh	11.00	85
Sai Study Circle Manual	20.00	210
Sri Sathya Sai Gita – All about Spirituality in Qs & As - P.P. Arya	42.00	485
The Essential Sai	39.00	410
The Glory of Womanhood	17.00	205
To my Father - Justice Padma Kastgir	24.00	165
Sai Echoes from Kodai Hills	20.00	235
Quiz on Bhagavatam	10.00	50
Quiz on Mahaabhaaratha	7.00	50
Quiz on Raamaayana	7.00	50
Quiz on the Bhagavath Geeta	7.00	35
Quiz on Divine Life of Bhagavan Sri Sathya Sai Baba	6.00	65
Raso Vai Sah - Brahmananda Panda	48.00	450
Sai Baba and You - Practical Spirituality - Mark and Barbara Gardner	27.00	295
Seeking Divinity - Dr. John S. Hislop	32.00	385
Thought for the Day	26.00	215
Divine Discourses on Easwaramma Day	18.00	225
Divine Memories - Diana Baskin	47.00	485
Unforgettable Baba - Joyce Darlene Barker	40.00	335
Aura of the Divine	37.00	435
Sree Gurucharanam (A Compilation of Guru Poornima Discourses)	11.00	145
Prema Dhaara Vol. 1(Letters written by Bhagavan to His students)	16.00	130
Prema Dhaara Vol. 2 (Letters / Messages from Bhagawan to His students / teachers and others)	29.00	325
The Light of Love	18.00	225
The Wish-Fulfilling Tree - Don Mario Mazzoleni	44.00	545
The Mind and its Mysteries	14.00	170
Truth is Only One	32.00	370
Prasanthi Nilayam Information Booklet	10.00	110
The Dharmic Challenge	25.00	335
The Direct Flight to Divinity	18.00	230

Dasara Discourses 1997 (Senses for Selfless Service)	15.00	160
Dasara Discourses 1998	19.00	200
Dasara Discourses 1999 & 2000	25.00	280
Dasara Discourses 2001	18.00	220
Dasara Discourses 2002	13.00	160
Dasara Discourses 2004	6.00	150
Dasara Discourses 2005	11.00	110
Message of the Lord	185.00	1575
Sathya Sai Parenting - Rita Bruce	33.00	390
Sri Sathya Sai Anandadayi - Karunamba Ramamurthy	48.00	550
Sri Sathya Sai Ved Vani - A compilation of discourses by Bhagavan Sri Sathya Sai Baba on Veda	50.00	560
Siva Sakthi Swarupa	13.00	130
The Mission of Sathya Sai at a Glance	70.00	430
Tribute	70.00	760
Vision of Sai I	47.00	465
Vision of Sai II	48.00	465
Who is a devotee of the Lord	12.00	85

FOR SALE ONLY IN INDIA

Transformation of the Heart - Judy Warner	28.00	285
Reconnecting the Love Energy - Phyllis Krystal	25.00	265
Taming our Monkey Mind - Phyllis Krystal	28.00	340
Suggestions for Study Groups and Individuals use of the Ceiling on Desires Programme	10.00	75
A Catholic Priest Meets Sai Baba - Don Mario Mazzoleni	34.00	490
Pathways to God Vol. I - Jonathan Roof	26.00	360
Pathways to God Vol. II - Jonathan Roof	39.00	385
Pathways to God Vol. III - Jonathan Roof	45.00	460
With Love Man is God - Samuel H. Sandweiss	115.00	755

Rates indicated are the prevailing rates. They are liable to change.

INLAND / OVERSEAS BOOK ORDERS

Books are despatched by Regd. Book Post only subject to availability. Indents and remittances within India should be received by Money Order/Indian Postal Order/Account Payee Cheques/Bank Drafts.

REMITTANCES

Remittances from Overseas towards Book Orders can be sent by A/C payee Bank Cheque / Demand Draft / International Money Order in **FOREIGN CURRENCY ONLY AND NOT IN INDIAN RUPEES.** Sending Cash Currency is liable to be confiscated by Government.

All remittances should be in favour of **THE CONVENER, SRI SATHYA SAI BOOKS AND PUBLICATIONS TRUST, PRASANTHI NILAYAM, ANANTAPUR DISTRICT, ANDHRA PRADESH, INDIA, PIN CODE - 515 134,** payable at State Bank of India, Prasanthi Nilayam (Branch Code No. 2786) mentioning full address in capitals with Area Pin Code, Zip Code No., where the books are to be despatched.

The approximate postage + packing + forwarding charges for Overseas Sea Mail and Inland per packet are indicated below:

Wt. of Packets	Overseas		Inland
	APPU Countries	Others	
Up to 500 gms.	Rs.78/-	Rs.82/-	Rs.37/-
Above 500 gms. - Below 1 kg	Rs.93/-	Rs.100/-	Rs.42/-
Above 1 kg - Below 2 kg	Rs.109/-	Rs.118/-	Rs.52/-
Above 2 kg - Below 3 kg	Rs.135/-	Rs.150/-	Rs.72/-
Above 3 kg - Below 4 kg	Rs.162/-	Rs.180/-	Rs.82/-
Above 4 kg - Below 5 kg	Rs.188/-	Rs.212/-	Rs.92/-

N.B. Maximum weight allowed per packet is 5 kgs. Weight of packing materials *per packet* to be added to the weight of books – Overseas – 300 gms.
Inland up to 2 kgs – 100 gms. Above 2 kgs and up to 5 kgs – 300 gms.
APPU Countries: Afghanistan, Australia, Brunei, Cambodia, China (People's Republic), Fiji, Indonesia, Iran, Japan, Korea (Rep.), Laos (Rep.) Malaysia, Maldives, Myanmar, Naura, Papua New Guinea, Philippines, Solomon Island, Sri Lanka, Thailand, Vietnam, New Zealand, Singapore.

***